Other Books by Donald G. Bloesch

FAITH

& ITS

COUNTERFEITS

DONALD G. BLOESCH

INTER-VARSITY PRESS
DOWNERS GROVE
ILLINOIS 60515

InterVarsity Press is the book-publishing division of Inter-Varsity Christian Fellowship, a student movement active on campus at hundreds of universities, colleges and schools of nursing. For information about local and regional activities, write IVCF, 233 Langdon St., Madison, WI 53703.

Distributed in Canada through InterVarsity Press, 1875 Leslie St., Unit 10, Don Mills, Ontario M3B 2M5, Canada.

All Scripture quotations unless otherwise noted are from the Revised Standard Version of the Bible, copyrighted 1946, 1952, © 1971, 1973, and are used by permission. Other versions quoted include the King James Version (KJV), the New International Version (NIV) and the New English Bible (NEB).

ISBN 0-87784-822-X

Printed in the United States of America

Library of Congress Cataloging in Publication Data

Bloesch, Donald G., 1928-
   Faith and its counterfeits.

   Includes bibliographical references and index.
   1. Apologetics–20th century. I. Title.
BT1102.B546   239   81-3704
ISBN 0-87784-822-X   AACR2

18	17	16	15	14	13	12	11	10	9	8	7	6	5	4	3	2	1
94	93	92	91	90	89	88	87	86	85	84	83	82	81				

Dedicated to the
St. Chrischona Pilgrim Mission
and the Basel Mission
(both in Basel, Switzerland)
where my two grandfathers received
their missionary training.

Acknowledgments

*I wish to express my deep
appreciation to my wife Brenda
for her immense aid in
copy-editing this manuscript.
I also wish to thank
Mrs. Peg Saunders, faculty
secretary of the University of
Dubuque Theological Seminary,
for her careful typing.
I am indebted to Mrs. Edith Baule
and Miss Lillian Staiger of our
theological library staff for their
assistance in procuring books and
other materials that were needed
for the completion of
this manuscript.*

For I desire steadfast love and not
sacrifice, the knowledge of God,
rather than burnt offerings.
Hosea 6:6

For the kingdom of God is not
food and drink but righteousness and
peace and joy in the Holy Spirit.
Romans 14:17

Our task is to take what the
Lord gives us—not to tire ourselves
out by worrying over what
he does not give us, but simply to
rejoice as we think what a great
God and Lord we have.
Teresa of Avila

A string of opinions is no more
Christian faith than a string of beads
is Christian holiness.
John Wesley

To deny oneself is to be aware
only of Christ and no more of self,
to see only him who goes before and
no more the road which is
too hard for us.
Dietrich Bonhoeffer

Preface

This is a handbook on evangelical spirituality that can be used by laypeople as well as by clergy and theological students. Its purpose is to show the difference between true Christianity and some counterfeit versions of the faith: legalism, formalism or ritualism, humanitarianism, enthusiasm, eclecticism and heroism. The Christian needs to be aware of these spurious forms of religion, since they all claim to be "the real thing."

Although it is common among evangelicals to distinguish between revelation and religion and to give precedence to the former (and this is entirely legitimate), I hold that there is such a thing as "true religion," a religion anchored in the gospel and dedicated to the glory of God. In the context of this study, religion is understood as the state of being grasped by an ultimate concern and the attempt to relate this concern to the whole of life. Because religion is basically a human enterprise, it is always fraught with ambiguity as a result of human sinfulness and finitude. It is also continually subject to the temptation to idolatry, in which human constructs and ideals take the place of the living God. Still I contend that our religious strivings, which are invariably egocentric, can be purified by the gospel and brought into the service of the kingdom of God (Jas. 1:27). Yet Christian religion is not immune to the human craving for power and security. Even a religion that appeals to the biblical revelation needs to be justified by the grace of God.

True religion will acknowledge that human salvation lies not in religion but in the outpouring of God's mercy as revealed in Jesus Christ. True religion is based not on man's ascent to God but on God's descent to man. Yet God's condescension to sinful humankind has as its purpose humanity's redemption and elevation. Justification has for its aim the *sanctification* of the sinner, which means conformity to the will of Jesus Christ. The religious enterprise at its best is God and man working in covenant partnership to bring all of life under the dominion of the gospel.

My hope is that this book will be helpful to our brothers and sisters in the historic Catholic churches as well as in evangelical Protestantism. It is often said in evangelical circles that both Roman and Greek Catholicism accommodated the Christian faith to classical philosophy so that the motivations and goals in religion were decisively altered. For example, it is alleged that the New Testament ideal of self-sacrificing love (Agape) was compromised in an attempted synthesis with the self-regarding love (Eros) of classical thought. It is also contended that the humanist ideal of happiness or interior well-being was incorporated into Christian faith without any drastic modification so that religion was given a decidedly anthropocentric orientation. Although there is some truth in these charges, it should nonetheless be recognized that a great many saints and mystics of the Catholic church drew on the resources of biblical faith far more than on classical philosophy. Some can be considered models of true spirituality, even in the evangelical sense. Catherine of Siena, for example, displayed a distinctly biblical stance when she relayed these words of her Master: "I have placed you in the midst of your fellows... so that you may love your neighbor of free grace without expecting any return from him, and what you do to him I count as done to me" (*Dialogue of the Seraphic Virgin*, chap. LXIV).

The lines between true and false religion will, I trust, become clear to the reader, particularly with regard to the current scene. It is generally acknowledged that much popular religion (both conservative and liberal) is narcissistic, focusing on inner feelings and on purely personal hopes and goals. God is deemed necessary to help his people attain the desires of their hearts or to find perfect happiness. Some even make the object of religion sound like capitalist consumerism—acquiring the goods of this life. But is prosperity an inevitable concomitant of true faith?

Against this anthropocentric kind of spirituality, I propose a theocentric spirituality which sees the glory of God and the advancement of his kingdom as more important than either material or spiritual gain for oneself. Not self-realization but the realization of our vocation as heralds and ambassadors of Jesus Christ should be our primary concern. We find our true selves only by losing ourselves in the cause of the kingdom (Mt. 10:39; Lk. 9:24-25; Mk.

8:35-37). When we make our chief concern the kingdom of God and his righteousness, the necessities of life will be ours as well (Mt. 6:30-33).

Franz Kafka once observed: "The Fathers of the Church were not afraid to go out into the desert because they had a richness in their hearts. But we, with richness all around us, are afraid, because the desert is in our hearts." Christians who are crippled by fear or doubt have either fallen away from the faith or have ceased to press forward to perfection. Such persons need a new anointing of the Holy Spirit so that they can resume the struggle to fulfill their holy vocation and at last attain the crown of salvation.

The church as a whole needs a fresh infusion of the Spirit of God in order to give a bold and clear witness to the divine mysteries of which it is a steward (Acts 4:31; 1 Cor. 2:1-5, 12-13). A church that has lost its first love, that has become lukewarm in its faith, requires a new heart and a new spirit (Ezek. 18:31). Only then will it be able to take the offensive against the powers of darkness, who have already been dethroned by the Lord of the church in his atoning death on the cross and his glorious resurrection from the grave. The heart of stone within the present-day church needs to be replaced by a heart of fire. The church must again become an agent of salvation rather than an obstacle to it. Before there can be a new world, there must be a converted church.

Therefore let this be a rule of discerning true religion; for surely that is true religion which doth make us go out of ourselves; that takes away all from ourselves and gives all the glory to God.
Richard Sibbes

There are plenty to follow our Lord halfway, but not the other half. They will give up possessions, friends and honors, but it touches them too closely to disown themselves.
Meister Eckhart

The taking of the cross means the death of self, of personal ambition and self-centered purpose. In the place of selfish attainment, however altruistic and noble, one is to desire alone the rule of God.
George Eldon Ladd

1
Religion That Glorifies God

FOR SEVERAL YEARS I PARTICIPATED in a prayer fellowship that met in the Chicago area. It was presided over by Charles Whiston, veteran missionary to China under the Episcopal church. Dr. Whiston is a remarkable intercessor, with a prayer list that has sometimes approached nearly two thousand names. He told us that each name was on a card and that he would go through those cards whenever the occasion permitted—on trains, planes, in bus depots and so forth—with often rewarding results.

One evening Dr. Whiston revealed that his prayer life had not always been so fruitful. For years he had begun his prayers with the words, "O Jesus, our great Teacher and Companion." That was the standard introduction for chapel prayer at Harvard University, where he had been a student. Many years later, on the mission field in China, it was indelibly impressed on him that Jesus was more than a teacher or prophet. He was the Savior of the world, the Lord of glory. In a small mission chapel in China, Whiston was suddenly moved to pray for the first time, "O Jesus, Lord and Savior." He then saw the significance of the apostle Paul's words in 1 Corinthians 12, "No one can say 'Jesus is Lord' except by the Holy Spirit" (v. 3).

Charles Whiston would be the first to acknowledge that before his awakening he had had a sense of the moral law of God, but was not yet in communion with God. He had practiced the externals of religion, but not until he had faith in the living Christ was he impelled to serve and glorify God out of love. Only then did he begin his sacrificial ministry of intercession. Eventually he embarked on a ministry of spiritual counsel. He became the spiritual director of Christian laypeople and clergy who needed the kind of assistance that only a great warrior of the faith could give.

Religiosity vs. Biblical Piety
Religiosity is not the same thing as biblical piety, nor is churchianity identical with Christianity. The mere practice of religion often promotes rather than alleviates guilt and anxiety. Scrupulous observance of the laws and codes of sacred tradition may grieve the Spirit. A beautiful liturgy may quench the Spirit. Scripture tells us that the only worship acceptable to God is worship "in spirit and truth" (Jn. 4:23-24; Phil. 3:3). We are urged not to believe every new voice but to "test the spirits to see whether they are of God; for many false prophets have gone out into the world" (1 Jn. 4:1). The sooner we sense the chasm between true and false religion, the closer we will be to authentic revival.

True religion is not simply keeping the law, but keeping the law in a spirit of love. It is not merely going to church, but going to church with a burning desire to adore the living God. It is not simply saying prayers, but pouring out one's heart before God, crying to God out of the depths. It is not clinging defensively to the doctrines of a particular church, but speaking the truth in the boldness of faith and the power of love. True religion is a work not just of sincere people but of Spirit-filled people, those who have been made beneficiaries of the grace of God.

The key to true piety is not to subscribe to the ethical teachings of Moses or of Jesus, nor is it to have the right perceptions of God and reality. Instead it is being united with Christ by faith and then living the kind of life that proceeds from that union. True piety means having a zeal for God's glory and a love for God's people. It means having a piercing and abiding sense of God's holiness and a passionate concern to serve the cause of his kingdom in the world. It includes both a horror of blasphemy and an awesome wonder at the infinite depths of the divine mercy demonstrated in the life, death and resurrection of Jesus Christ. True piety issues in a morality of obedience motivated by a desire to glorify God in all areas of life.

Popular religion commonly depicts happiness as the goal of the Christian life. Biblical faith sees happiness as a by-product but not the goal of the Christian life; the primary goal is the glorification of God and conformity to his will. As Christians we are called to *holiness*, not *happiness*. At the same time, in our quest for holiness we shall find true happiness.

It is also helpful to draw a distinction between *happiness*, understood as the satisfaction of the desires of the heart, and *blessedness*, the state of being reconciled with God and neighbor. It is not wrong for us to seek the satisfaction of our innermost desires as a secondary goal in life's pilgrimage so long as we pray for their transformation and recreation. Grace signifies not merely the fulfillment of human longings and strivings but also their negation. To desire one's own happiness above all else is a crudely eudemonistic form of religion. To seek first the glory of God is biblical religion. Those who dedicate themselves to God's glory and to the ministry of reconciliation are *blessed*, even though contentment in life may at times be taken from them. They may even have to endure grave hardships, including persecution.

Popular religion is incurably egocentric: it is intent on gaining for the self a place in the sun. In that perspective, faith is an investment guaranteeing security in this life and in the life to come. In the biblical view, faith is a reckless abandonment of self-interest. It is taking up the cross and following Christ wherever he might lead us, sometimes against our own hopes and inclinations.

Not the gaining of the world but the denial of the self is the hallmark of Christian ethics. The motivation in denying ourselves, moreover, is not to earn our salvation. Nor is it to extricate ourselves from the encumbrances of worldly obligations. Instead, the aim of the life of faith is to subordinate self-interest to the glory of God and the welfare of our neighbor. The priority for the Christian is God first, our neighbor second and the self last. We are not to neglect concern for self-betterment, but the Bible is clear that this must not become our paramount concern.

Recovering the Sacred
Behind the doctrinal confusion, the emptiness in worship and the moral anarchy of our times lies a loss of the sacred or holy in our lives and in the life of our culture. The frantic attempts of some people today to shore up biblical author-

ity and confessional or denominational loyalty attest to a dissipation of real contact with the divine presence whom we know as the God and Father of our Lord Jesus Christ. Efforts to bring God down to our level, to see God as "pal" or "brother" or even "sister" instead of Master and Lord, likewise underscore his absence. Such efforts invariably end in worshiping a construct of God rather than the living God himself.

The recovery of the sacred depends on a new initiative from God, on a fresh outpouring of the Holy Spirit in which fellowship with God is reestablished through acknowledgment and repentance of sin, both personal and social, and through a new venture in obedience to the divine commandment. A renewed love for the Scriptures will also be reflected in the recovery of the sacred. This will be manifested not simply in Bible study but in an ardent desire to bear witness to the biblical, evangelical proclamation in our words and deeds. Grace will become real for us again when we risk our very lives and reputations for the sake of the gospel.

It is for freedom
that Christ has set us free.
Stand firm, then,
and do not let yourselves
be burdened again by
a yoke of slavery.
Galatians 5:1 NIV

If the Spirit of grace
is absent, the law
is present only to accuse
and kill us.
Augustine

For *love* is the only
meaning of the law:
therefore *obedience*
to the law can only be
an *echo or response*
to God's love.
G. C. Berkouwer

2
Legalism

IN THE EIGHTEENTH CENTURY, John Wesley, noted for his emphasis on the use of the law as a guide for Christian living, had to be constantly on the alert for outcroppings of legalism among his followers. On one occasion Wesley had lunch with a gentleman whose daughter, a person of remarkable beauty, had been singularly impressed with Wesley's preaching. One of Wesley's fellow preachers, a man of plain manners and little tact, noticing that she wore a number of rings, suddenly took hold of her hand and raising it asked his colleague: "What do you think of this, sir, for a Methodist's hand?" The young woman was profoundly embarrassed, and the question was awkward for Wesley, known for his aversion to jewelry. But the aged evangelist answered with a quiet, benevolent smile, "The hand is very beautiful." That evening the young woman appeared at the gospel service without her jewelry and committed her life to Christ.

This vignette shows Wesley as a man of evangelical wisdom; he answered in the spirit of our Lord, not as a legalist. Early Methodism was noted for its emphasis on personal holiness as well as on the Reformation doctrine of salvation by grace, but for the founders of Methodism, John and Charles Wesley, holy living never became a pretext for a new legalism.

Lost Vitality

How often vital religious movements once characterized by freedom of the Spirit have become defensive, hypercritical and legalistic in the second and third generations! Consider the Quakers in seventeenth- and eighteenth-century England. At the beginning of their history, they boldly carried the gospel throughout the land despite ostracism and frequent martyrdom. But within a relatively short period of time the original fervor began to ebb. They became embroiled in issues having more to do with codes of behavior than with the substance of faith. Their pressing concern became to maintain their identity. Faith was transformed from an adventure into a duty. As some members became lax in their faith, others, alarmed at the growing worldliness, sought to keep their treasure safe within a clever cage of rules. One of the controversies among these later Quakers was whether they should have tombstones over their graves!

That which is really the law of God should indeed be taken seriously, for the law was given to remind us of our sin and direct us to the path of holiness. Yet the peril confronting all religion that emphasizes the law's importance is *legalism*, which means depending on our own efforts toward righteousness rather than on the righteousness that God makes available to us in Jesus Christ. The "natural man" desires to make himself acceptable before God by cultivating piety or by zealously fulfilling the requirements of the law. The gospel, however, proclaims the joyful news that God accepts us while we are still sinners. He forgives us even though we fail in our attempts to make ourselves righteous. True religion is believing that God accepts us despite our sin—so long as we trust not in ourselves but in him who came to rescue and liberate us from sin.

Once the love of Christ breaks into our lives, we are moved to give of ourselves for our neighbor's welfare and salvation. We then strive to keep the commandments, not in order to earn or guarantee our salvation (as in legalism), but as a token of our gratefulness for what God has done for us in Jesus Christ. We become motivated to live righteous lives by a desire to glorify God in everything we say and do.

Legalism appears in many guises. When it takes the form of a misguided dogmatism, holding right doctrine is made a condition for salvation. As a false asceticism, legalism sees works of self-effacing piety as meritorious in God's sight. In the guise of rigorism, it makes the rules governing religious life into inflexible principles instead of guidelines needing constant reassessment in the light of God's self-revelation in Jesus Christ.

Legalism or moralism is a relationship to a moral code rather than to a living Savior. It knows only the law's requirements, not the love that goes beyond the law and thereby fulfills the spirit of the law. In legalism keeping the law becomes an end in itself rather than a means to the service of God and fellow humanity.

Jesus' Attack on Legalism

Jesus was especially vehement in his denunciation of legalism. His angriest words were aimed at the Pharisees, who regarded adherence to the prescriptions of Judaic law as the epitome of righteousness. The Pharisees practiced tithing and said many prayers, but neglected justice and the love of God (Lk. 11:42). When Jesus healed on the sabbath and befriended moral outcasts, the Pharisaic party rightly saw that he was breaking with legalistic religion. Seeing him as a threat to their way of life, they accused Jesus of being "a glutton and a drunkard, a friend of tax collectors and sinners!" (Mt. 11:19).

Jesus denounced the Pharisees as men who "trusted in themselves that they were righteous and despised others" (Lk. 18:9). He made clear that his mission was "not to call the righteous, but sinners" (Mt. 9:13). In order to see, he declared, we must first acknowledge that we are spiritually blind, that our righteousness is illusory when viewed in the light of the perfect holiness of God. Only those who admit they are blind will begin to see, whereas those who think they see will end up in blindness (Jn. 9:39-41).

Against the legal righteousness of the Judaic tradition, Jesus proclaimed the spiritual righteousness of the kingdom of God that exceeds the righteousness of the scribes and Pharisees (Mt. 5:17-20). In his view, we must not only not kill, but refrain from hateful words and actions. We must not only not steal, but even renounce the right to reparations for wrongs we have suffered. The Pharisees taught the principle of "an eye for an eye and a tooth for a tooth," but Jesus taught the principle of no retaliation (Mt. 5:38-39; Rom. 12:14-21; 1 Pet. 2:23). Jesus internalized or radicalized the law. The difference between the two kinds of righteousness is the difference between fulfilling an obligation and showing sacrificial love. It is the difference between adhering to a moral code and living out costly discipleship under the cross. Jesus acknowledged that "with men" his ethic of radical love "is impossible," but "with God all things are possible" (Mt. 19:26).

Paul's Break with Legalism

Paul, too, turned against legalistic religion, but only after he was confronted by the risen Christ on the road to Damascus and was moved to repentance and faith. Paul was a stout defender of the Pharisaic tradition until his eyes were opened by the Spirit. Then he saw that salvation lies in God's gracious condescension to man in Jesus Christ, not in man's ascent to God through satisfying the requirements of Mosaic Law. For Paul, Christians are no longer under the law of sin and death but are now under the direction of the Spirit of life who leads them into the higher righteousness.

The essence of true religion is aptly summarized in Romans 5:1-5: "Since we are justified by faith, we have peace with God through our Lord Jesus Christ. Through him we have obtained access to this grace in which we stand, and we rejoice in our hope of sharing the glory of God." Paul went on to say that "hope does not disappoint us, because God's love has been poured into our hearts through the Holy Spirit which has been given to us" (v. 5). This theme was reaffirmed by the apostle in Romans 14:17, where the spiritual roots of the faith are united with ethical concern: "The kingdom of God does not mean food and drink but righteousness and peace and joy in the Holy Spirit." The same note of optimism is sounded again in Romans 15:13, where Paul says, "May the God of hope fill you with all joy and peace in believing, so that by the power of the Holy Spirit you may abound in hope."

The gospel, according to Paul, offers deliverance from the burden of the law by which we must reap the consequences of our wrongdoing. The good news is that Christ has reaped the burden of sin and guilt in our place and that salvation is therefore free to all who avail themselves of it through faith in his atoning blood. Once we have been inwardly awakened to the reality of God's mercy shown to us in Christ, we come to realize an inner peace and heartfelt joy sustained by an abounding and unshakable hope. That hope is strengthened by the joy and peace that spring from a lively faith in Christ.

Paul made unmistakably clear that the gospel liberates from all religious and moral legalisms and taboos. Many Jewish Christians were still insisting on Sabbatarian laws, the rite of circumcision and adherence to Old Testament injunctions against unclean foods. Some Christians influenced by ascetic movements were tempted to practice vegetarianism. Others in the community of faith were reluctant to eat food that had been offered to pagan deities before it was put on the market. Paul did not wish to offend those who had scruples about such things as eating meat and drinking wine, so he advised that in the company of such people it was better to abstain (Rom. 14:21). But inwardly, he said, we are free from such taboos (Col. 2:16-17). The gospel message is redemption through the grace of Jesus Christ, not by works of the law.

The essence of faith is communion with God and righteousness, peace and joy in the Holy Spirit (Rom. 14:17; 15:13). True religion does not consist primarily in outward observances, or in moral rectitude, or even in relationships that demonstrate genuine friendliness or fraternity. Instead, it is an inner assurance that God is with us. It is a supreme confidence that his grace is sufficient to overcome all obstacles to faith and all barriers to fellowship. It is char-

acterized by an invincible faith in the holy God and an un-
quenchable love for our fellow human beings based not on
mutual attraction (as in friendship), but simply on the desire to serve without any expectation of personal gain or
reward.

It is well to keep in mind that Paul was not speaking in
either Romans 5 or 14 about people's awareness of their
own righteousness or about what they can do on their own
apart from the grace of God. Instead he was referring to the
righteousness of faith, which must indeed be reflected in
the lives of believers. This righteousness is imputed to us
on account of our faith in Jesus Christ. But it also takes
root in us by the power of the Holy Spirit. It therefore fur-
nishes the basis of our sanctification, the ongoing process
of purification completed only at death. The righteousness
that comes from God must be evident in our dealings with
other people, particularly our brothers and sisters in the
household of faith (Rom. 14:15—15:6). Whatever actions in
our lives do not proceed from faith, God regards as sinful
(Rom. 14:23).

The peace that Paul was upholding is not the peace of
mind or absence of tension so often adulated today. Nor is
it the freedom from adversity promised by the false prophets of new religions. Instead, it is the knowledge of divine forgiveness available only to self-confessed sinners.
The peace imparted to those who believe is an assurance of
being reconciled with God through the sacrifice of Jesus
Christ (Rom. 5:1). It connotes restoration to the favor of
God, even though we may well be out of favor with the
world. As we saw in Romans 14:17, it also signifies being
reconciled with other Christians by the work of the Holy
Spirit. Such peace persists amid storms of life that can shat-
ter our mental and emotional equilibrium. It endures
when we must take issue with brothers and sisters in the

faith or even vigorously oppose them. It is a peace that the world simply cannot understand (Phil. 4:7; Jn. 14:27), since it comes to us not through satisfaction in personal accomplishment, but through despair of ourselves and trust in God's mercy.

Once we throw ourselves on God's mercy we will experience the joy of which Paul writes: gladness in knowing that our sins are forgiven and confidence that we will share in the future glory of God. Such joy is constantly renewed by the certain hope that God will not disappoint us, that he will remain true to his promises. It is quite different from what the world means by "happiness," a comfortable life with realization of earthly gain. This joy can be our possession even when loved ones or the necessities of life are taken from us. In the midst of personal tribulation and anguish, even in sickness and at the verge of death, the believer can still have the joy that the Holy Spirit brings, the radiant assurance that Jesus Christ is an everpresent refuge and that he will come again in glory to bring to his own the crown of salvation.

Luther's Discovery

Paul had to break with legalism in order to come to a saving relationship with Christ. In the sixteenth century, Martin Luther likewise had to break free from the oppression of moralistic religion to gain peace with God. As a monk in the Augustinian cloister in Erfurt, Germany, and then at the Augustinian house at Wittenberg, he had led a life of exemplary piety and rigorous spiritual discipline. But he was inwardly in torment. Not until he pored over Paul's epistle to the Romans was he suddenly awakened to the true meaning of the gospel: it is by faith alone that the just shall gain life (Rom. 1:17 NEB).

Luther then saw his monastic works of piety as filthy

rags in God's sight. Instead of gaining merit he was insuring his own perdition by seeking to guarantee salvation for himself by an ascetic lifestyle. Luther was struck by the realization that the "righteousness from God" revealed "in the gospel" (Rom. 1:17 NIV) is not God's punitive righteousness, which condemns sinners to hell. It is God's forgiving righteousness, by which in his mercy he makes sinners "just." Luther described his breakthrough into a new horizon of meaning: "Then it seemed to me as if I were born anew and that I had entered into the open gates of Paradise. The whole Bible suddenly took on a new aspect for me."[1]

Luther's so-called evangelical discovery compelled him finally to leave the cloister, although his release from monastic vows resulted more from the pressures of ecclesiastical politics than from his personal desire. He was led by the Spirit to go out into the world proclaiming the good news that God justifies the ungodly, that by grace through faith we are pardoned from sin—not because of moral achievement or devotional rigor. Luther did not denigrate works of piety or spiritual exercises, but he steadfastly denied that they played any role whatever in our justification before God. We are justified not by our good works, which are never good enough to merit God's favor, but by Christ's perfect work, his atonement on the cross, which we lay hold of by faith. Because of Luther's refusal to compromise on what he knew to be the essence of the gospel, he was excommunicated by his church and condemned by the emperor to a life that included exile and persecution.

Christian Liberty
The Reformation, associated with Luther, Calvin and Zwingli among many others, signified a recovery of the

apostle Paul's understanding of Christian liberty (Rom. 6:15-19; 1 Cor. 6:12; Gal. 5:1-15). Such liberty is not anarchy but the freedom to obey God as we are guided by a conscience bound to his Word. This freedom is to be contrasted with every style of life or mode of behavior that connotes bondage to human traditions (Mk. 7:9-13). Nearly all the Reformers married, many of them seeing their marriages as signs or parables of Christian liberty. For the most part, they allowed for the possibility of a vocation to lifelong celibacy, but they refused to view it as a meritorious work and rejected it as a law that the church could impose on its ministers. In his *On Monastic Vows*, Luther wrote, "Marriage is good, virginity is better, but liberty is best." (When marriage becomes mandatory or virtually mandatory, especially for the clergy, as has been true in many Protestant circles since the Reformation, the ideal of Christian liberty is again subverted.)

It is important, of course, not to fall into the opposite heresy, antinomianism, which Paul also condemned (Rom. 6:1-4; 1 Thess. 4:1-7). We must not make the mistake of thinking that we can live without the law. Christ did not come to abolish the law, but to fulfill it (Mt. 5:17). At the same time, in his work of fulfillment he pointed beyond the letter of the law to its innermost meaning: love toward God and neighbor. The law by itself cannot save; it can only accuse and condemn. When we enter into the "grace and truth" that come through Jesus Christ (Jn. 1:17), we are set free to live according to the basic intention of the law, that is, in the spirit of love.

By striving to keep the commandments we honor Christ who suffered and died to save us from sin, death and hell. At the same time, we need to remember that our imperfect works of love must be covered by the grace of Christ. Our justification as well as our glorification are assured to us through faith in his righteousness, which alone merits for us eternal salvation. Our endeavor to live a holy life becomes a witness and sign of the perfect holiness of Christ, which alone entitles us to heaven.

It is not enough
to know Christ as crucified
and raised up
from the dead,
unless you experience,
also, the fruit of this.
John Calvin

For what is holiness
according to the oracles
of God?
Not a bare external
religion, a round of
outward duties,
how many soever they be,
and how exactly soever
performed. No:
gospel holiness is no less
than the image of God
stamped upon the heart.
John Wesley

The trouble with
some of us is that
we have been inoculated
with small doses
of Christianity
which keeps us
from catching
the real thing.
Leslie Weatherhead

3
Formalism

THE PREACHING OF JOHN TAULER, a fourteenth-century Rhineland mystic, exemplifies the need for constant renewal in the Spirit. Although he had attained a certain fame as a preacher in Cologne, Tauler's sermons lacked the fervor and simplicity that characterize preaching in the power of the Spirit. On one occasion he asked a spiritually wise layman to give an honest report of his preaching. The layman replied that Tauler was preaching out of pride, as did the Pharisees. Instead of becoming hostile or reproachful, Tauler placed himself under the layman's guidance for a period of silence and seclusion. He then received a special visitation from God's Spirit that gave him new vigor and confidence. For a time he seemed to have lost all sense and reason. His lay counselor said this about the change that occurred: "As formerly the letter had somewhat killed thee, so now shall the same make thee alive again. For now thy teaching comes from God the Holy Ghost, whereas before it was from the flesh."[1] Tauler returned to his pulpit to become a great winner of souls. He had previously preached what was generally considered sound doctrine, but now he preached with ardor and power. He had experienced a personal encounter with the Holy.

Deadly Enemy

Formalism is a deadly enemy of true religion. Formalists accept the doctrine without the spirit and embrace the forms of godliness without the power (2 Tim. 3:5). Formalists are preoccupied with propriety in worship and theology. Their attention is fixed on the celebration of holy days rather than the call to holy obedience (Gal. 4:10). They are more concerned with "ritual sacrifice" and "burnt offerings" than with the sacrifices of broken and contrite hearts (Ps. 51:17; cf. Amos 5:21-24; Mic. 6:7-8; Hos. 6:6). Formalists appeal to church traditions rather than to the Word that speaks anew in every age, judging and reforming tradition (Mt. 15:6). Formalistic preaching may be orthodox, but it is devoid of the power of the Spirit and the conviction of faith (1 Thess. 1:5). Formalistic prayer consists of thoughtless repetition or perfunctory liturgical recitation lacking spiritual depth.

The demise of fervent congregational singing is one of many indications of creeping formalism in churches today. When hymns become liturgical exercises and music is valued more for aesthetic appeal than for its witness to the truth embodied in Jesus Christ, the Spirit is being quenched and grieved. When a choir or paid performers preempt congregational singing or when a choir's main function is to demonstrate artistic skill rather than to as-

sist congregational singing, the people in the pew have become spectators instead of participants in worship.

The liturgical movement has sought to bring congrega-
tions into more active and meaningful participation in
worship services, but unison and responsive readings,
litanies, sung responses and genuflections are no substi-
tutes for prayers from the heart and singing under the conviction of the Spirit. A unison prayer of confession may
provide an occasion for true repentance, but it may also
foster the illusion that such repentance has necessarily occurred. Recitation of creeds may enhance worship celebra-
tions by enabling a church to reflect on its heritage, but if
such recitation falls short of being a bona fide personal
reaffirmation of faith, it only testifies to the erosion of spiritual vitality in a congregation.

Just as liberalism gravitates toward humanitarianism
and an amorphous mysticism, so orthodoxy's temptation
is legalism and formalism. When formalism intrudes into
orthodoxy, whether in ritualistic worship or prayer or in
unloving dogmatism, religion becomes lifeless and bur-
densome. Orthodoxy understood as outward assent to
correct doctrine can even turn a church's dogmatic formu-
lations into idols.

Liberal Christianity is also susceptible to the encroach-
ment of formalism, but this is more apparent in the areas of
worship and church order than of doctrine. Liberalism,
rejecting limitations imposed by dogmas or creeds, has
been remarkably open to enthroning liturgical forms along
with church programs and polity. It has also been tempted
to absolutize the ethical precepts of religion, thereby pre-
paring the way for a new moralism.

When the forms of tradition are separated from their
life-giving source, the living Word of God, they are either
discarded for something new or invested with the aura of

divinity. The forms and symbols of the faith then become graven images to which we give homage that should be reserved only for God (Ex. 20:4-6). We should not be blind to the fact that dogmatic or creedal symbols can become graven images as easily as liturgical symbols.

Many who have lost the faith of their forebears or who have experienced a crisis of faith have become rabid denominationalists, confessional polemicists, high church ritualists or simply latitudinarians willing to live and let live. Such persons are also inclined to become theological faddists, swayed by the latest ideologies penetrating the church from the culture. With the erosion of faith, demons enter to fill the spiritual vacuum in the soul.

The Centrality of Faith

True religion consists neither in fidelity to traditions of the church nor in religious decorum, though such things may be salutary, but in single-minded, wholehearted devotion to a living Savior. Right doctrine is included within the purview of true religion, but faith transcends doctrine.

Holding right beliefs is not inconsequential. Jude warned, "Contend for the faith which was once for all delivered to the saints" (v. 3). In Titus we read that a bishop "must adhere to the true doctrine, so that he may be well able both to move his hearers with wholesome teaching and to confute objectors" (1:9 NEB; cf. 2:1; 2 Thess. 2:15; 1 Tim. 1:3-4; 2 Tim. 1:13-14).

Yet right doctrinal formulas, however necessary for the integrity of worship and theology, are not in themselves decisive for salvation. When the jailer in Acts 16 came to the point of despair, he knelt down before Paul and Silas and cried out, "Men, what must I do to be saved?" (v. 30). Paul's answer was clear and forthright: "Believe in the Lord Jesus, and you will be saved, you and your household" (v. 31). The only prerequisite for salvation is faith, which is not so much intellectual assent as venture and trust in the certainty that God will provide (Rom. 5:2).

Faith, to be sure, includes knowledge. We could not believe in Jesus Christ unless we had been told who he is and what he has done for us. Faith also seeks understanding. Theology is indispensable in the life of the church; a church cannot exist apart from a theological explication of its foundational message. Paul was writing theology in all his letters, and particularly in his letter to the Romans, and it is these books that form the touchstone of biblical doctrine.

Ritual, too, is important. Could there be a church without liturgy, sacraments and symbols? Fellowship seldom maintains itself without institutional forms. The preached Word needs to be supplemented by the visible Word (the sacraments) to create and shape the kind of enduring community that we call the church. Yet true religion is deeper than ritual, externals and creeds, less abstract than theology. Faith has an interior quality. It is a relationship of inwardness to a living Lord (Rom. 14:22). It is more weighty than an outward pledge of allegiance. It involves a life-and-death decision.

It is not enough to have the externals of religion. We must experience its power. It is not sufficient to give lip service to right doctrine. We must demonstrate the genuineness of our doctrine by the practice of a holy life. It is not enough to believe the truth. Truth must take root in our hearts and lives.

Certain Samaritans who had been told by a woman about Jesus sought him out to ascertain whether he was the promised Messiah (Jn. 4:28-42). When they were confronted again by the woman they declared, "It is no longer because of your words that we believe, for we have heard for ourselves, and we know that this is indeed the Savior of the world" (Jn. 4:42). Nothing can take the place of this inner spiritual knowledge given by God himself.

Orthodoxy is necessary for the integrity of faith, but if it is not anchored in and sustained by personal devotion to Jesus Christ, it degenerates into a dead orthodoxy. The written code or the letter of the law without the spirit kills (2 Cor. 3:6), although the spirit needs the letter as a vehicle for its full manifestation. What is required is a live orthodoxy, a living faith which is not a doctrine about Christ but a relationship with Christ.

It should be an occasion for joy when we hear that our brothers and sisters are following the truth (3 Jn. 4), but it may also be a cause for concern if their enthusiasm does not proceed from faith working through love (Rev. 2:4). John warned the church in Ephesus that in its zeal to promote sound doctrine and to stamp out heresy, it had lost its first love: inward devotion to Jesus Christ manifested in love for other Christians (Rev. 2:2-6). The church at Ephesus was commended for opposing the antinomian heresy of the Nicolaitans, yet love for sound doctrine must not be pursued at the expense of love for God and neighbor. Churches that have maintained the traditions of the faith but are no longer in an abiding communion with Jesus Christ need to pray: "Wilt thou not revive us again, that thy people may rejoice in thee? Show us thy steadfast love, O LORD, and grant us thy salvation" (Ps. 85:6-7).

Pascal's Transforming Encounter
Another Catholic luminary like John Tauler whose faith was transformed from intellectual adherence into personal commitment was Blaise Pascal, a brilliant mathematician and scientist in seventeenth-century France. Pascal first experienced what might be described as a conversion to

the church through encounters with the Jansenists, a biblically oriented Catholic fellowship. He soon became a defender of orthodoxy and even helped to secure the condemnation of a heretical teacher. Yet his faith was not solidly anchored, and for a time he succumbed to the distractions of worldly life.

Then one evening as Pascal was reading the seventeenth chapter of John's Gospel, his room was suddenly filled with the flaming presence of Christ; under the conviction of sin he resolved to live wholly for his Savior and Lord. His experience was so overwhelming that Pascal carried a record of it sewed in the lining of his coat—found only after his death. He then abandoned his worldly pursuits. After selling his coach and horses, his fine furniture and silverware, he gave all the proceeds to the poor. He discarded even his extensive library, keeping only a few devotional books and the Bible. The glory of his Savior became his only concern. Before he had been converted to the right theology; now he was anointed to the apostolate of souls. Before he had affirmed the cross and resurrection of Christ; now he personally experienced crucifixion and resurrection (cf. Rom. 6). Whether this experience was his true conversion or a "second blessing" deepening his initial commitment is a matter of dispute. What is undeniable is that his keen interest in the Bible and theology kindled by the Jansenists had not been sufficient to save him from spiritual aridity and quiet desperation. The renewal of spirit he had been earnestly seeking was now given to him.

Pascal is best remembered for his *Pensées* ("Thoughts"), a powerful apologetic for the Christian faith, which stands in sharp contrast to rationalistic apologetics. Particularly striking is that not Pascal's own experience but the Christ whom he experienced shines forth from its pages. Pascal, like Calvin, sought to give God all the glory.

Francke's Dramatic Awakening

The conversion of August Hermann Francke in the late seventeenth century is also illustrative of the break with formalism into a vital, evangelical faith. Raised in a pious Lutheran home, Francke studied theology at the University of Leipzig but confessed that he had strayed from "the former good beginning of a true Christianity" which he had in his childhood. Though attending church services and participating in confession and Communion, he still did not have inner peace or joy: "I grasped my theology in my head and not in my heart, and it was much more a dead science than a living understanding."[2] The Bible study group that he was in stressed the scientific approach.

An invitation to preach in St. John's Church in Lueneburg proved decisive for the realization of his vocation to be an ambassador of Jesus Christ. He planned to preach a sermon showing how a "true, living faith" differs from a "mere human and imagined faith." Yet this attempt brought home to him the fact that he himself lacked the very faith that he was to urge upon his hearers. A powerful battle raged within him, which was to continue for several days. As he put it: "I again fell on my knees . . . and cried to God, whom I neither knew nor believed, for salvation from such a wretched condition." It was then that he experienced the assurance, joy and peace that he had been seeking, and he rose praising and magnifying his Lord and Savior. "As I knelt down," he said, "I did not believe there was a God, whereas when I got up I would have confirmed it without fear or doubt."[3]

From this personal encounter with the living Christ, Francke discovered a new power in his life to preach and witness with courage and boldness. No longer did he have a desire for honor in the academic community or for status among the nobility. His foremost desire now was simply to uphold Jesus Christ in the service of the lost and needy of the world. Francke demonstrated the genuineness of his conversion by founding an orphanage, homes and schools for the very poor (including poor girls, which was an innovation) and a Bible institute for the publication of the Scriptures. He never dwelt upon his conversion, though he referred to it on occasion. His focus was on God's great mercy shown forth in Jesus Christ, and his conversion was a signpost that always reminded him of the unmerited forgiveness of a gracious and loving heavenly Father.

Bonhoeffer's Inner Revolution

Dietrich Bonhoeffer, the German Lutheran pastor executed by the Nazis toward the end of World War 2 for subversive activities against the German state, is also indicative of the tension between true religion and formalism. In spite of his mastery of theology and scholarly understanding of Scripture, demonstrated in the sermons he delivered in formal church gatherings, in the early period of his ministry he still did not have a personal acquaintance with the living Christ. He later confessed: "I plunged into work in a very unchristian way. An... ambition that many noticed in me made my life difficult.... Then something happened, something that has changed and transformed my life to the present day. For the first time I discovered the Bible.... [Formerly] I had often preached, I had seen a great deal of the Church... but I had not yet become a Christian."[4]

Only after this "momentous inner revolution" did Bonhoeffer discover the reality of prayer. Before that, he had seldom if ever prayed in the sense of heartfelt petition to a personal, living God. He began a systematic meditation on the Bible that was entirely different from the exegetical and homiletical treatment of Scripture to which he had been exposed in the course of his theological studies. Moreover, he began speaking of auricular confession not as a theological concept, but as an act to be carried out in practice.

Bonhoeffer became a source of inspiration to fellow pastors in the German resistance against Hitler. Even in prison he manifested an inner joy and radiance that rekindled the hopes of other prisoners. The prison doctor gives this picture of Bonhoeffer on the day of his execution: "Through the half-open door of a room in one of the huts I saw Pastor Bonhoeffer, still in his prison clothes, kneeling in fervent prayer to the Lord his God. The devotion and evident conviction of being heard that I saw in the prayer of this intensely captivating man moved me to the depths."[5]

Bonhoeffer did not plead for a churchless or purely spiritual Christianity. Yet he saw that the forms of the faith, including the church itself, are empty husks unless the Spirit breathes on them and opens the inner eyes and ears of those who are exposed to these forms. Even the Bible remains a dead letter until the Spirit reaches out through the words and touches the hearts of those who read and hear. Only then can the Bible be referred to as the sword of the Spirit that delivers from sin and death (Is. 49:2; Eph. 6:17; Heb. 4:12; Rev. 1:16).

New Wineskins

Can the new wine of the gospel be poured into the old wineskins of church tradition (Mt. 9:17; Lk. 5:37-39)? Are new forms needed to hold the new wine of the Spirit? Certain forms were instituted by Jesus Christ, such as the sacraments, the Lord's Prayer and the preaching of the Great Commission. If we discard such forms, which contain the promise of new life, we risk severing our relation with biblical faith itself. The same can be said for the Bible, which is uniquely inspired by the Spirit of God and designated as an abiding means of grace (Ps. 119:105; Jn. 10:35; 17:17; Rom. 16:25-26; 2 Tim. 3:14-17). On the other hand, liturgical and creedal forms that do not have dominical sanction may have to be revised or discarded if they become impediments to new light breaking forth from God's Word. Even iconoclasm may be legitimate in certain periods of church history, when outmoded, meaningless or idolatrous forms need to be swept away so that the pure Word of God can again be heard.

When the prophet Ezekiel pondered the question, "Son of man, can these bones live?" (Ezek. 37:3), he was told that Israel's heritage could be resurrected and endowed with new power. That answer implied that Israel's worship would have to undergo purgation and revision (Ezek. 37:23). Jesus made clear that the forms of Judaic religion, unless decisively altered, could not hold the new wine of the gospel (Mt. 9:15-17). The church today faces an uncertain future. Perhaps through a new confession of faith and new forms of worship and hymnody, standing in continuity with the past, it will be enabled to bring a fresh and vibrant witness to the living Christ for our time.

The soul of the care
of the poor
is the care
of the poor soul.
Teresa of Avila

To reconcile man with man
and not with God
is to reconcile no one
at all.
Thomas Merton

The anti-Christ will come
disguised as the great
humanitarian. He will
talk peace, prosperity,
and plenty—not as
a means to lead us to God,
but as ends in themselves.
Bishop Fulton J. Sheen

4
Humanitarianism

IN THIS DAY ESPECIALLY, it is important to remember Jesus' words to the crowd who followed him after he had multiplied the loaves and fishes: "Do not labor for the food which perishes, but for the food which endures to eternal life" (Jn. 6:27). Salvation lies in receiving the bread of life, not in the promotion of worthy causes or in social welfare programs, however important these things may be on their own level.

Humanitarian Concerns
True religion should not be confused with humanitarianism, no matter how similar they may appear. The object of humanitarianism is not to identify with the world in its shame and affliction (Jas. 1:27), nor to permeate the world with the leaven of the gospel, but to remold the world in

the image of enlightened humanity.

Humanitarianism is a liberal form of religion emphasizing service to humanity above all other concerns. Since the self is included in humanity, there is always a keen interest in serving one's own welfare as well. The goal is the greater happiness of man, not the glory of God. Although it is inclined to make a place for the *assistance* of God in realizing purely human ends, humanitarianism embraces many who maintain an agnostic or even atheistic stance.

In humanitarianism the emphasis is not on keeping the law as a condition for salvation (as in legalism) but simply on service to the community as a sign of our magnanimity and good will. Charitable service is done not to win merit in the sight of God but to ease human conscience in the face of social wrongs and to achieve a sense of human brotherhood.

Humanitarian service in itself may well be a good thing, but it is not the same as the righteousness that comes from faith working through love (Gal. 5:4-6). When concern for social improvement pre-empts the hope for the righteousness of the kingdom, we are in the humanitarian rather than the biblical thought-world. The focus is no longer on the deliverance of humanity by a divine Savior but on rebuilding humanity. While the humanist seeks only to improve the world, the evangelical seeks a new world, a new heaven and a new earth.

In true religion, the power of faith brings to us unsuspected possibilities moving us to go beyond the call of duty. People who have faith love others to the point of weariness without any expectation of return. People oriented to this world love in order to gain their own happiness or salvation, even when serving others. Or they love in order to demonstrate their own virtue or the virtue resident in humanity, of which they are a part. People of faith love even their enemies, seeking the good of those who persecute and malign them (Rom. 12:14-21). People oriented to this world are willing to help those who aspire to a better life, but they seldom if ever serve those who threaten their own values or security. Truly religious men and women will confess that after having done all, they are still unworthy servants (Lk. 17:10) because they regard themselves only as sinners who have been used by God.

The humanist knows little or nothing of the love that reaches out to the poor and despised without any ulterior motive. For the ancient Greeks, love understood as Eros proceeds upward to divinity, not downward to humanity in its frailty and brokenness, as does Agape or Christian love. Eros seeks its own good or perfection, while Agape seeks the good of the undeserving neighbor. Eros is self-enriching and self-elevating whereas Agape is self-emptying. Eros means realizing one's own fulfillment in God and with the aid of others; Agape means making oneself expendable for God and for others.

When Christians in the early and medieval church accommodated to classical philosophy, it was commonly said that people should love the divinity reflected in their neighbor—but not their neighbor as a sinful human being. But biblical faith proclaims that God loves this world, even in its fallenness, that he justifies not the righteous but the ungodly (Rom. 4:5; 5:6). Our Lord by no means wishes the world to remain in its sin, but his love reaches into the world even in its sin. Luther put this dramatically: "Rather than seeking its own good, the love of God flows forth and bestows good. Therefore sinners are attractive because they are loved; they are not loved because they are attractive. . . . This is the love of the cross."[1]

Under the impact of the eighteenth-century Enlightenment, the golden rule (Mt. 7:12) was rephrased: Act always so that you respect every human being, yourself or another, as a rational creature. But do self-respect and respect for others do justice to the biblical conception of love?

Christian Love

Love in the biblical sense is compassion that embraces sinners in their misery, not toleration that respects others despite their sin. Love is less a rational esteem than a holy madness driving one to sacrifice one's own interests and welfare for the good of others. Love in the Christian sense is not prudent and calculating but ecstatic and overflowing, or as Bernard of Clairvaux put it, "impetuous, vehement, burning."

Such love impelled Mary Magdalene to bathe the feet of her Lord in perfume and her own tears (Lk. 7:37-47). When Catherine of Genoa ministered to victims of the plague as a nurse, she kissed a stricken woman on the lips without regard to her own safety. Francis of Assisi extended the hand of friendship to lepers he had disdained before his conversion; filled with the Spirit of God, he embraced them with tears of love.

Christian love goes beyond moral obligation or rational expectation. It transcends and may even appear to contravene moral justice and paternalistic altruism. Humanitarian love is often prompted by concern to share the fruits of enlightenment. A genuine Christian, on the other hand, is willing to give up enlightenment for the sake of others. Humanitarians try to raise the less fortunate to their own level; Christians are willing to descend to the level of the unfortunate.

People who donate time and money to community projects, who work to improve social conditions, fulfill their obligations as responsible citizens. Yet such people are not necessarily Christian. No "good works," however exemplary, make people Christians. Christianity is not do-goodism, though true faith will impel us toward good works through gratitude for what God has done for us in Christ. True religion must not be reduced to ethics, but it is the wellspring of all creative moral endeavor. True religion will manifest itself in uprightness in life and in a willingness to forgive and be reconciled.

The gift of faith is accompanied by an outpouring of love into our hearts by the Holy Spirit (Rom. 5:5). Faith must be fulfilled in love, just as justification must be fulfilled in sanctification. At the same time, love rests on faith, as sanctification rests on justification. Faith alone justifies; love attests that faith is alive. Faith is personal; love is social. Faith is the foundation of the Christian faith; love is the goal. Faith is the root; peace, joy and love are the fruits.

Humanists ignore divine love and the faith implanted in human beings by God's Spirit. Their concern is with a purely human love, a kind of righteousness that human beings can accomplish through their own efforts. If men and women were perfect, our works of love might indeed assure us of God's favor or bring peace to our conscience; it is sin, infecting every part of our being, that makes our love and righteousness so lacking in God's sight (Is. 64:6). Even for those of us who call ourselves disciples of Christ, spiritual love is invariably mixed with natural or self-serving love. The only righteousness that can save is the righteousness assured to us through faith in the blood atonement of Jesus Christ. It is faith in his righteousness that cleanses from sin. Our love is a sign of his love and his righteousness (1 Jn. 4:10-11).

Many humanists find support in Micah 6:8: "What does the LORD require of you but to do justice, and to love kindness, and to walk humbly with your God?" At first glance,

Micah seems to advocate a purely ethical religion or even "salvation by works." Yet we see that in its context this verse is based on the proclamation of God's free grace: "I brought you up from the land of Egypt, and redeemed you from the house of bondage" (v. 4). The people of Judah were enabled to obey the commandments of God because they had been delivered by the grace of God.

True Religion

The essence of true religion is presented in Micah 7:7: "As for me, I will look to the LORD, I will wait for the God of my salvation; my God will hear me." Seeking the will of God in prayer should precede works of loving-kindness and mercy. The fruit of faith is good works; the soul of faith is prayer.

The great saints of the church have revolutionized society because they have given the world a new metaphysical vision, a world and life view anchored in the transcendent. They have provided not simply programs for social change, but a sense of meaning and purpose to existence. They have instilled in all sorts of people a zest for living and a spirit of adventure. The Enlightenment, which gave birth to modern rational religion as well as to secular humanism, taught people to remain within their natural limitations and not to aspire to saintly heroism.[2] Yet in the same period of history, many evangelicals risked their reputations and lives to bring an end to the slave trade and to child-labor abuses. Christians also spoke out forcefully against sea piracy, the liquor traffic and social conditions that bred poverty.

What the world most needs is not *nice* persons but *new* persons, men and women with a new vision of life and drastically changed motivations and goals (2 Cor. 5:17; Gal. 6:15). Neither law-abiding citizens, philanthropists, nor social reformers as such can create a holy community characterized by both the fear of God and the equitable treatment of society's members. It is men and women whose sights are on the transcendent city of God who can best move the world toward a higher degree of righteousness. This is because they seek to make people free without making them sacrilegious. They agree with Augustine that while order is based on justice, justice is based on piety.

Humanitarianism seeks to have *morality* (service to one's neighbor) without *piety* (submission and surrender to God). The problem is that morality bereft of the fear of God often degenerates into attempts to manipulate one's neighbor for one's own ends. True piety invariably leads to moral action on behalf of others. Moral action may or may not lead to piety.

César Malan

César Malan was a nineteenth-century Swiss pastor of Huguenot ancestry whose sermons to his Geneva congregation lacked power and biblical content. Despite his ordination pledge "to preach the pure gospel of our Lord Jesus Christ," he later confessed that he had been "an entire stranger to the evangelical doctrine of salvation by grace." The rational religion taught at his seminary had emphasized human virtue, not divine grace.

At the urging of evangelical friends Malan began searching the Scriptures. One passage made an indelible impression on his soul, Ephesians 2:8-9: "For by grace you have been saved through faith; and this is not your own doing, it is the gift of God—not because of works, lest any man should boast." In the classroom where he taught Latin, Malan pondered the implications of these verses one day, then suddenly rose and walked about the college court saying to himself, "I am saved."

On Easter 1817, Malan, preaching in the Church of the Madeleine in Geneva, announced his new faith. His parents were shocked. (His father was an admirer of the humanist philosopher Diderot.) Fellow clergymen under the spell of Enlightenment rationalism turned against him, finally succeeding in barring him from the pulpits of Geneva. Although his wife was deeply grieved, Malan would not renounce his newfound faith. Outside the city in a small village he built a Chapel of Witness, and in the power of the Spirit his ministry took on new dynamism. People came to hear him from all over Europe. Once he had proclaimed the truths of "natural religion"; now he uttered the Word of God, which is like a fire devouring all that stands in its path or a hammer that "breaks the rock in pieces" (Jer. 5:14; 23:29). Malan's ministry sparked a revival that helped to preserve the evangelical witness in the Swiss Reformed church, whose founding fathers had been Calvin and Zwingli.

William Booth

Christianity has an ethical mandate, but it cannot be reduced to ethical humanitarianism. We see that in the life and witness of William Booth, who with his wife Catherine founded the Salvation Army. As an earnest young man dedicated to Christ, Booth wanted to serve the downtrodden in English society, especially the most wayward derelicts of the slums. On one occasion, however, when he brought a group of ragged youths to a middle-class Methodist worship service in Nottingham, the minister had the outsiders removed from the main portion of the sanctuary to avoid disturbing more respectable churchgoers. Because intense class prejudice permeated the churches of England at that time, William Booth was compelled to develop a new form of ministry addressing itself to the needs of the poor. The East London Revival Mission, which he and his wife organized, later became the Salvation Army.

William Booth was thoroughly convinced of the integral relationship of faith to social welfare and reform, but he did not see social service as the essence of true religion. While agreeing with humanitarians that people need bread to survive, he recognized that people "shall not live by bread alone, but by every word that proceeds from the mouth of God" (Mt. 4:4). He was acutely aware that unless physical and material needs are met, our hearers may be in no condition to understand and pay heed to the gospel we proclaim. General Booth's motto was "Soup, soap and salvation," but he never confused soup or soap with salvation (which is a current temptation).

Mother Teresa

Today many know of a remarkable Roman Catholic nun, Mother Teresa, founder of the Missionaries of Charity who minister to the poorest of the poor in the slums of Calcutta and other cities in India. Her "Homes for the Dying" serve the incurably ill who would otherwise die on the streets. Although some hail Mother Teresa's work as a noble experiment in humanitarianism, she insists that her overriding purpose is to bring poor people to God. She believes that when we identify with their affliction and loneliness in self-giving love, the poor will see the love of Jesus Christ who died for the sins of the world. Without that evangelistic motivation, she says, "our work would just be social work, very good and helpful, but it would not be the work of Jesus Christ."[3] She says emphatically: "Faith is a gift of God. Without it there would be no life. And our work, to be fruitful, and to be all for God... has to be built on faith."[4]

Mother Teresa seeks to alleviate the "material poverty" of the desperately poor and homeless. But above all she is concerned about their "spiritual destitution." She reminds us that although we have many medicines for all kinds of physical afflictions, there is no cure except love for the devastating experience of being unwanted. Such love comes from Jesus Christ and reaches the world through those united to Christ.

While her emphasis is on the hidden apostolate of prayer and on witnessing by Christian presence, Mother Teresa nonetheless sees a place for spoken witness. The heart of missionary work is to "tell everyone the news that the kingdom of God has come." Yet she insists: "The essential thing is not what we say, but what God says to us and through us. All our words will be useless unless they come from within—words which do not give the light of Christ increase the darkness."[5]

Corrie ten Boom

Corrie ten Boom is another model of Christian sanctity in our time. Because of her role in the resistance movement in Holland, hiding in her own home persecuted Jews sought by their Nazi oppressors, she was arrested and imprisoned. At the infamous Ravensbruck concentration camp for women in Germany, where 97,000 died, Corrie and her sister Betsie brought spiritual strength and consolation to their fellow prisoners. In a dormitory where the fleas and lice were so numerous that the German guards dared not enter, she and her sister conducted illegal prayer meetings and Bible study for despairing and destitute women. Her sister died in prison from beatings and malnutrition. Corrie, whose health had become precarious and who was marked for execution, was miraculously freed from the camp through a clerical error.

After the liberation of Holland a few months later, Corrie ten Boom became "a tramp for the Lord," traveling throughout the world with the good news of salvation through the atoning blood of Jesus Christ. She testifies that she was able to survive her prison ordeal, including solitary confinement, only because the love of Jesus enabled her to forgive her captors. Like the German evangelical pastor Johann Christoph Blumhardt a century before, she took as her motto "Jesus is Victor."

Corrie ten Boom has united social service and evangelism in her ministry. Shortly after the war she reopened her father's watch shop, taking in mentally retarded people who sought her care and protection. With the Sisters of Mary, a Protestant community in Germany, she converted an internment camp in Darmstadt into a home for refugees. The rehabilitation center for ex-prisoners and other war victims she founded in Bloemendaal in the Netherlands now receives people from all walks of life in need of rest and care. For a time she ministered to leprosy patients in Taiwan. She has visited prisons in more than forty countries giving words of encouragement and consolation, especially to the condemned on death row. When the man who had betrayed the ten Booms to the Nazis was caught after the war and sentenced to die, Corrie wrote to him. She made clear that she forgave him for what he had done to her and her family, and asked him to turn to Christ to receive God's forgiveness.

Even before the war, Corrie ten Boom had been involved in a ministry of Christian service. Having accepted Christ as her Lord and Savior at age five, she thereafter devoted herself to the welfare of others. Besides working with the mentally handicapped in Haarlem, her home town, she founded and directed a club that provided teen-age girls with opportunities for recreation and spiritual training.

Corrie ten Boom's principal vocation has been that of a "soul-winner," leading the spiritually lost into a saving relationship with Jesus Christ. Seeing herself as only a feeble instrument in the hands of God, she recognizes that it is primarily through the gospel proclamation that people are liberated from bondage to sin, guilt and the devil. She testifies: "We are called to be God's ambassadors, His missionaries, the light of the world in a time of chaos and great darkness. And as we see chaos and darkness increasing, our responsibility also increases."[6]

Our Greatest Service

Although Good Samaritan service sometimes has chronological priority over evangelism, the mission of the church is not fulfilled until we declare the message of reconciliation and redemption. The highest service we can render other human beings is to direct them to the bread of life, the living bread which comes down from heaven (Jn. 6:32-58). Love is most fully demonstrated in introducing lost sinners to Jesus Christ (1 Cor. 9:22; 2 Cor. 4:5-6; 5:11-15). Faith calls us to self-giving service, but we should never forget that the work most pleasing to God is believing in his Son, Jesus Christ (Jn. 6:29; 17:3; Phil. 3:8-9; 1 Jn. 3:23; 5:4-5).

The mistake in humanitarianism is in equating the spiritual and the secular so that the worship of God becomes nothing other than the service of humanity. Yet we must beware of falling into the opposite error of Gnostic religion by positing a dichotomy between the spiritual and secular, by trying to escape from the secular into the spiritual. In line with Hebraic holism, evangelical Christianity insists on the inseparability of the spiritual and the secular, but gives priority to the spiritual. Service to humanity is not a substitute for worship of the living God, but it is the crowning fruit and evidence of a right relationship with God.

You should not believe
your conscience and
your feelings more than
the word which the Lord
who receives sinners
preaches to you.
Martin Luther

I know no state of soul
more dangerous than
to imagine we are born
again and sanctified
by the Holy Ghost,
because we have picked
up a few religious feelings.
Bishop J. C. Ryle

Be ruthless with yourself
if you are given to talking
about the experiences
you have had. Faith that
is sure of itself is not faith;
faith that is sure of God
is the only faith there is.
Oswald Chambers

5
Enthusiasm

AUGUSTINE, A TOWERING FIGURE among the church fathers, was blessed with various mystical experiences, including his conversion experience in a garden outside his lodging in Milan, Italy. Hearing what he thought was a child's voice saying "Take up and read," he found a Bible on a nearby table and opened it at random to Romans 13:13-14. In this passage Paul warns against reveling, drunkenness, immorality and jealousy, urging his hearers to "put on the Lord Jesus Christ, and make no provision for the flesh, to gratify its desires" (v. 14).

Keenly aware that this text spoke to his condition, Augustine sensed God's presence breaking into his life. Up to that time he had led a life of debauchery, having had several mistresses and an illegitimate son. Now he found himself delivered from bondage to his passions through a joyous awakening to faith in Jesus Christ. A light of serenity shone in his heart; the darkness of doubt vanished away; he had become a new person (2 Cor. 5:17).

Augustine had tasted of the glory that is to come, but he also knew the darkness of faith when one has to do without experiential support and consolation. When mystical allurements are absent, he said, "I do not seek them, and when they are present, I do not reject them, but I am prepared to do entirely without them."[1]

Religious Enthusiasm

Understanding the difference between true religion and religious enthusiasm is especially needed in our time. Religious enthusiasm (from the Greek *en theos*, meaning literally "in God") is the quest for a direct or immediate experience of God. It includes the dimension of ecstasy, which means being taken out of oneself into God. Enthusiasm upholds the ecstatic experience of God over Scripture, tradition and the creeds. It is closely related to, if not synonymous with, the heresy of spiritualism, which locates authority in the spirit or inner light as opposed to Scripture and the church.

Enthusiasts seek after a premature redemption, a dramatic anticipation of the glory that is yet to be revealed. Not content to wait for the revelation of God's glory on the last day, they desire to be taken up into that glory now. They often look for signs and wonders to corroborate the claims of the gospel. They see themselves not as pilgrims journeying to a foreign land, but as initiates into the higher mysteries of the faith. Instead of servants of the One who alone *has* the truth and *is* the truth, they want to be spiritual masters who already have access to the secrets of the kingdom. They point not beyond themselves to Christ crucified and risen, but to their own experience. The public revelation in the Bible is subordinated to their own private revelations, which often come in the form of dreams and visions (Jer. 23:25-32).

Many great saints of the church like Augustine had graphic encounters with the divine. Yet they did not make them the norm for their teaching and preaching, as enthusiasts do. Those saints were led out of their experiences and out of themselves into the service of the kingdom. They could persevere in faith apart from miraculous events and seldom based the truth of their message on such events.

True religion acknowledges faith as an experience as well as trust and commitment. Yet faith is deeper than mere experience, just as the righteousness of faith is more basic than our awareness of that righteousness. When we venture forth into darkness, we know in our hearts, even without experiential supports, that God is with us, that his Spirit will sustain us. Faith is more fundamental than feeling, but includes feeling. To say, as some do today, that we can have faith without experiencing the love of Jesus Christ or the joy and peace of the Holy Spirit is nonsense. The invasion of the Spirit's reality into our lives affects our senses as well as our will.

Coming to faith includes an experience of the love of God and the joy of salvation, but the life of faith is not a seeking after great experiences. It is taking up the cross and following Christ in costly discipleship. The Christian life consists in obedience: the "work of faith," the "labour of love" and the "patience of hope" (1 Thess. 1:3 KJV). Its goal is not to possess God in ecstatic experience but to obey God in righteous living. People of faith need to draw close to God in mystical communion (Ps. 34:8), but the object is to conform our wills to the will of God as we serve him in the world. It is not to make ourselves divine.

Many extol the "born-again experience" or the experience of "Holy Spirit baptism." Yet salvation does not consist in the *experience* of new birth but in the *fact* of new birth. Invisible and intangible, the new birth is actually something beyond our sensate experience, although it has a decided effect on our reason and senses.

It is not wrong to seek the peace and joy that Christ brings so long as we accept his searing judgment on us and his lordship over us. Our primary concern is to be united with Christ by his Spirit, not to gain the benefits of exhilaration that proceed from such a union.

Whatever our experience of the new birth or encounter with Jesus Christ, it must not be made a standard for others. That was a pitfall of the Corinthian church, which raised speaking in tongues to a sign or guarantee of higher spirituality. Paul had to combat that misunderstanding by emphasizing the ethical fruits of the Spirit as evidence for the genuineness of faith (1 Cor. 13; 2 Cor. 6:6-7; 8:7; Gal. 5:22-26). He did not denigrate extraordinary gifts of the Spirit or ecstatic experience. Far from being a rationalist theologian, he claimed to have spoken in tongues "more than all of you" (1 Cor. 14:18 NIV). He spoke of having received many visitations of the Spirit (2 Cor. 12:1-7). Nonetheless, he resisted the temptation to make such experiences the badge of being a Christian. They formed neither the basis for his certainty of salvation nor the focus of his preaching (2 Cor. 4:5).

There is obviously a place for personal testimony in Christian witness. Jesus told a man who had been delivered from demon-possession to return to his village and tell what had happened to him (Lk. 8:39). Paul spoke of his conversion when testifying before the Jews at Jerusalem and before Agrippa and Festus (Acts 22:6-11; 26:12-18).

Our testimony can be a prelude to the gospel if we point beyond our own experience to the God who has acted in Jesus Christ for the salvation of the world. At the same time, we must relate the gospel to concrete life and experience in the world.

A Pilgrimage of Faith

True religion insists that we are justified not by our experience but by faith, which is only an empty vessel holding the alien righteousness of Christ. Yet it is by the action of the Spirit that Christ's justification makes contact with us, and this means that no one can have faith without experiencing the living God. The felt presence of God's Spirit in our lives is not to be downplayed. At the same time, we must beware of basing our hope and confidence in ecstatic experience or mystical rapture instead of on the biblical promises concerning Jesus Christ and his church. We should not seek a direct vision of God in this life; we are called to embark on a pilgrimage of faith. And faith means hoping in the midst of despair, believing even when our senses testify otherwise, persevering even when we are assaulted by horrendous temptations.

Augustine warned against provoking God to anger by demanding from him "signs and wonders" and desiring those things, not for "some wholesome purpose," but only for the "experience of them."[2] Our sole hope and confidence, he believed, lie in the mercy of God, not in mystical raptures. Like his mentor Paul the apostle, Augustine was content to walk by faith alone and not by sight (2 Cor. 5:7).

Martin Luther, too, placed emphasis on faith over ecstatic experience. He asked his Lord to spare him from visions and raptures on his earthly pilgrimage, considering himself unworthy or unready for such outpourings of glory. In his opinion, the highest stage of faith is when

God hides himself from us so that we must venture forth in the darkness trusting only in his promises: "This is real strength, to trust in God when to all our senses and reason He appears to be angry; and to have greater confidence in Him than we feel."[3] Yet Luther also confessed to having experienced the joy, peace and confidence that faith brings. He declared that no one can understand the mystery of God's grace "without experiencing, proving and feeling it."

Those who seek an experience of God beyond what faith offers are trying to transcend their human limitations. True religion stands opposed to a "super-spirituality" that denies the continued frailty and sinfulness of the people of God. Growing in Christ brings an increasing awareness of our unworthiness and a deepening dependence on his righteousness alone for salvation. It should also bring visible progress (visible to others, not to ourselves) in the continuing battle against sin and renewed determination to go on to perfection (Phil. 3:12; Heb. 6:1, 11-12; 12:14).

Enthusiasm often prepares the way for antinomianism, a delusion that one is already perfected and therefore no longer subject to the restrictions of the law. Christians, though set free from the law's penalty, are still under the law's imperatives. No longer under the law of sin and death, we are now under "the law of Christ" (1 Cor. 9:21; cf. Rom. 8:2; 2 Jn. 6). As sinners, we who have faith still need the law to remind us of our sin and drive us again to the gospel of God's free mercy. As born-again believers, we stand in need of the law as a guide for Christian living. We are *justified* despite our inability to live up to the requirements of the law. Yet we are not *sanctified* apart from works of outgoing love that partially fulfill the spirit of the law.

True religion consists not in instantaneous total cleansing, but in a conversion that issues in still further conversions. To be sure, we do not grow into the kingdom; we enter through the crisis of a personal faith-decision. This critical turning point in life may or may not take the form of a cataclysmic experience. It will always come as the dawning of a new consciousness, but it may take place over a limited period of time; even then, however, it entails a decisive break with the past.

The decision to place our trust in Christ is only the beginning, not the end, of our spiritual pilgrimage. The whole Christian life is a continual turning from the way of sin to the way of righteousness. Justification does not simply set us on the way but is the rock to which we have to return if we are to be kept on the way. No matter how much progress we make, we always stand in need of God's forgiveness. Even as Christians, we must be reminded to "lay aside that old . . . nature" and "put on the new nature" (Eph. 4:22-24 NEB; cf. Ps. 51:10-12). Even sanctified Christians need to repent and begin the struggle anew. Scripture promises that God is always ready to forgive again, a promise that is confirmed to us by the interior witness of the Spirit.

Struggle and Victory

Enthusiast-Christians tend to stress victory in the Christian life but minimize the struggle. Others, standing closer to the Reformation, focus on the struggle but not on the victory. It is clear that we cannot share in Christ's glory unless we also share in the battle against sin and death (Rom. 8:17, 36-39; 1 Pet. 5:9-10). The theology of the cross and the theology of glory belong together.

That the Christian life entails both struggle and victory is evident in Romans 7 and 8, where Paul documents his own breakthrough into freedom. Paul was unhappily aware that the power of sin and death was constantly at work to draw him back into the state of bondage from which he had been delivered. He confessed, "I do not do the good I want, but the evil I do not want is what I do" (Rom. 7:19). "Who will deliver me from this body of death?" he asked despairingly (Rom. 7:24). Recovering his confidence he exclaimed, "Thanks be to God—through Jesus Christ our Lord!" (Rom. 7:25 NIV). In Romans 8 Paul declared that "through Christ Jesus the law of the Spirit of life set me free from the law of sin and death" (v. 2 NIV). Because we have the Spirit of God dwelling in us, we can persevere and overcome. In and of ourselves we are miserable sinners. But in Christ we can be "more than conquerors" because divine grace is more powerful than the law of sin and death (Rom. 8:37).

Luther and Calvin

Luther, tormented by the temptation to despair, would shut himself up in his room to wrestle with the powers of darkness assailing him. Even his wife could not gain access to him at such times. When his soul was thus troubled, he would meditate on the Psalms, for him a source of strength and consolation. From one of his bouts with the demon of depression came the words of his celebrated hymn, "A Mighty Fortress Is Our God." Though often cast down, Luther emerged triumphant by persevering in trust and hope, knowing that God would never totally abandon his children to the power of evil.

Steadfast fidelity to God in time of trial was also characteristic of John Calvin. In his prominent position in the Reformed church in Geneva, he was maligned by libertines who resented his zeal in upholding the law of God. His enemies also included many whose sympathies still lay with Rome. Dogs were set at his heels, guns were fired outside his house, angry fists hammered at his door, and loathsome songs were sung under his window. When he and two of his associates were finally banished, Strasbourg, where he was able to obtain a pastorate, seemed like a refuge.

Ironically, within a few years Calvin received a call to return to Geneva, where the authority of the Reformed church was near collapse. His first reaction is recorded in a letter to his friend Farel: "I would submit to death a hundred times rather than to that cross on which I had daily to suffer a thousand deaths."[4] Finally he submitted: "It is my desire that the Church of Geneva shall not be left destitute. Therefore I would rather venture my life a hundred times over than betray her by my desertion."[5] Calvin placed the glory of God and the welfare of God's people over his own comfort and happiness. As a result, he became one of the shining lights of the Protestant Reformation and an enduring influence on theology and on the moral and cultural life of nations.

John Calvin's faith was anchored not in feelings or past experiences (though he had had a sudden conversion), but in the biblical promises that God would provide in time of need. That is why he was able to persevere when the odds against him seemed insurmountable. After being confronted by an armed mob, Calvin wrote to his colleague Viret: "Believe me, I am undone unless God stretch forth his hand."[6]

Teresa of Avila

At about the same time that Calvin was solidifying the gains of the Protestant Reformation in Geneva, Teresa of Avila was spearheading a reform of the Carmelite order in Spain. After spending twenty years as a cloistered nun, much of that time in spiritual turmoil, she received what she later described as a "second conversion." While praying before a statue of Christ being scourged, a deep inner peace came to her followed by visions and other paranormal experiences. Some of them filled her with joy, others with terror. Gradually she came to realize that the purpose of those revelations was to deepen and renew her spiritual life and to empower her for the work of reform to which she was called. Although mystical experiences persisted throughout her life, they occurred less frequently in her later years—after her mission had been accomplished.

Despite the rapturous blessings she received, St. Teresa insisted that the essence of Christianity does not lie in mystical experiences, but in willingness to suffer for the sake of Christ. As she put it, "We must not show ourselves to be striving after spiritual consolations; come what may, the great thing for us to do is to embrace the Cross."[7] Indeed, "the highest perfection" consists not "in feelings of spiritual bliss nor in great ecstasies or visions nor yet in the spirit of prophecy" but in bringing our "will into conformity with that of God."[8]

A common temptation of mystics is to elevate their own experience of the divine presence over external authorities such as the church and Scripture. Interior voices and visions are often uncritically accepted, while the counsel of brothers and sisters in the faith is disregarded. Teresa sometimes questioned whether her visions were divinely inspired and surmised that if one received such visions in humility, then even if they came from the devil they could do no harm. On the other hand, if humility were absent, they could do no good, even if they came from God.

Teresa acknowledged that occasionally conflict occurred between her private illuminations and her spiritual director, who sought to instruct her in the light of Scripture and sacred tradition. In prayer the Lord would tell her to submit to her spiritual director,[9] but the Spirit then invariably proceeded to change the director's mind if misleading advice had been given. In this way Teresa was able to harmonize the word of her confessor, which she felt bound to obey, and the illumination of the Spirit, which came to her in prayer.

Martin Rinkart

An outstanding example of persevering faith in the next century was Martin Rinkart (1586-1649), pastor of the Lutheran church in Eilenberg, Saxony, during the Thirty Years' War. Ministering in a time of grave suffering for his people, he often lacked food for his own family. The walled city of Eilenberg became a city of refuge for victims of famine and plague. In 1637 eight thousand people in the city died of disease; in one year Rinkart buried four thousand of his parishioners. Finally he was the only pastor left in town, twice saving his city from the Swedish army which sought to impose exorbitant taxation. Though he died a worn and broken man in 1649, he never lost the inner assurance of his salvation.

In the midst of severe tribulation Rinkart proclaimed that "the Lord is good" and that "his mercy is everlasting" (Ps. 100:5 KJV). He was convinced that the Lord would keep his people "in his grace" and would "free us from all ills in this world and the next." Out of profound gratitude he composed that great hymn of consolation, "Now Thank We All Our God." His faith was not the response of an enthusiast who must taste God's glory before believing. Instead, Rinkart was like the biblical prophets who walked in darkness yet trusted in the name of the Lord and relied on their God (Is. 50:10-11). His was the light of faith, the light that is veiled to natural sight and reason.

The hallmark of true religion is not a secret knowledge

(higher than simple faith) or rapturous experience, but *freedom*—freedom to venture forth in faith and love wherever Christ might lead us. Paul said that wherever the Spirit of the Lord is, there is freedom (2 Cor. 3:17). To be free we must act in freedom, which we can do only through the power of grace working in us (Phil. 2:12-13). True freedom is not freedom to do as we please but voluntary submission to Jesus Christ (Rom. 6:15-23). Our will is not our own: it belongs to him who died and rose again for us so that we might have life that is abundant and fruitful in self-giving service.

We know God only by
Jesus Christ.
Without this mediator
all communion with God
is taken away.... Apart
from Jesus Christ,
we do not know what is
our life, nor our death,
nor God, nor ourselves.
Blaise Pascal

A gospel which is not
exclusive will never
include the world,
for it will never master it.
No religion will include
devotees which does not
exclude rivals.
Peter T. Forsyth

It is not surprising... if
the Christian who is in
some measure alive,
even though he be
sincerely open and
patient, must always give
to the non-Christian...
the impression of unfitting
and culpable intolerance.
Karl Barth

6
Eclecticism

German Protestants have witnessed in recent decades the rise of the No Other Gospel movement, which takes a firm stand against efforts of theologians and church leaders to bring the gospel into accord with modern scientific opinion. The No Other Gospel movement is especially concerned with those groups that are bent on "demythologizing" the Bible, which is tantamount to denying the reality of the supernatural. Some so-called enlightened scholars, for example, claim that Jesus' healings were likely the result of the power of suggestion. They regard the nature miracles as symbols of universal abiding truths. To their minds the miracle of the changing of water into wine (Jn. 2:1-11) supposedly illustrates the power of grace to transform the human spirit.

I still remember how one of my professors in a religion class at college tried to explain away the miracle of Jesus walking on water. He calmly assured us that Jesus was in all probability walking on a sandbar not visible to his disciples. But this would imply that Jesus deliberately deceived Peter in inviting him to walk on water (Mt. 14:22-33). With interpretations such as these, the primary appeal is to the norm of scientific rationality.

The Scandal of Particularity

A perennial temptation for Christians who seek to come to terms with the surrounding culture is to bend the gospel to fit the preconceptions of the culture. The first casualty in this kind of accommodation is the scandal of particularity, the biblical claim that God has revealed himself fully and decisively in Jesus Christ alone. Because this claim is a scandal to Greeks and folly to Jews, the church that seeks the praise of the culture is compelled to assert that the gospel represents only one truth among others—the highest truth, but not the only truth about God. Or it is led to assume that the gospel is one way to salvation—the best way, but not the only way. It is tempted to draw on the truth claims of other religions and philosophies in order to build its case for the gospel. Its point of departure is no longer divine revelation but religious and moral humanity.

Historians of religion have called the attempt to draw from a wide variety of traditions in order to arrive at a consensus "eclecticism." Eclectics desire to appropriate what is best in all systems of truth and refuse to follow any one system exclusively. They seek to be fair to all and therefore yield to all. Eclectics are similar to latitudinarians, who disdain doctrinal or creedal particularity. While eclectics seek to learn from all creeds, latitudinarians care little about particular creeds. For latitudinarians sincerity is more important than what is believed. Both eclectics and latitudinarians uphold the spirit of religion over dogma, the quest for truth over a definitive witness to the truth. Eclecticism is also associated with syncretism, which is the attempt to unite or reconcile opposing theological or philosophical positions. Sometimes the goal is to find a common denominator. At other times it is to arrive at a higher synthesis.

Eclecticism along with humanitarianism is one of the major temptations of liberal Christianity, though eclectic tendencies can be seen in conservative Christianity as well. It is not wrong to try to discern partial truths in non-Christian systems of thought, truths that need to be sifted and corrected in the light of Holy Scripture. But it is wrong to abandon the dogmatic truth claims of the faith in order to bring them into harmony with non-Christian religions or secular philosophy. Eclecticism, like humanitarianism, promotes doctrinal indifferentism, since what is valued is not dogma but life or experience. Eclecticism finally leads either to humanism, where rational dogma is reduced to ethics, or to mysticism, where rational dogma is dissolved in mystery.

If we examine the Bible carefully, we see that nowhere are the people of God urged to accommodate or adjust their beliefs to those of the surrounding culture. The Old Testament prophets were especially adamant that the religion of Israel be kept free from the taint of the idolatrous religions of the Canaanites and other tribes. Elijah, in opposing the attempts of Ahab and Jezebel to come to terms with Baal worship, spoke for all the prophets: "How long will you waver between two opinions? If the LORD is God, follow him; but if Baal is God, follow him" (1 Kings 18:21 NIV). Amos posed this crucial question: "Can two walk together, except they be agreed?" (3:3 KJV). For the prophets of Israel, the religion of the one true God does not confirm or fulfill, but rather displaces the false religions of sinful humanity.

This attitude continues into the New Testament. Jesus offended even the more open-minded Jewish scribes by his claim that he embodied the fulfillment of messianic prophecy and that he was the only doorway to salvation. His words, as recorded in the Fourth Gospel, were uncompromising: "I am the way and the truth and the life. No one comes to the Father except through me" (Jn. 14:6 NIV; cf. 10:7-10). Peter declared to the Jewish leaders in Jerusalem: "Salvation is found in no one else, for there is no other name under heaven given to men by which we must be saved" (Acts 4:12 NIV). Paul insisted, "No other foundation can any one lay than that which is laid, which is Jesus Christ" (1 Cor. 3:11). He especially emphasized the scandal of the cross: "For Jews demand signs and Greeks seek wisdom, but we preach Christ crucified, a stumbling block to Jews and folly to Gentiles" (1 Cor. 1:22-23).

In the early postapostolic period the catholic faith struggled with various heresies that drew heavily on philosophical sources in the pagan culture. Athanasius led the battle against Arianism, which denied the real incarnation of deity and which emphasized works over grace in the plan of salvation.[1] Irenaeus was among those who warned against the heresy of Gnosticism, which combined Christian ideas with mythological and philosophical themes drawn from a wide variety of sources. Gnosticism was eclecticism par excellence, since it sought to bring together Orientalism, Judaism, Hellenism and Christianity. In trying to incorporate Christianity into an eclectic vision, the Gnostics surrendered the biblical claims that the world was a special creation of God and that Jesus was the Son of God in human flesh.

The Battle between Luther and Erasmus

At the time of the Reformation, the battle against eclecticism reappeared in Luther's conflict with Erasmus, the noted Renaissance scholar. Erasmus issued an edition of the Greek New Testament in 1516 and in the preface urged that the New Testament be translated into all the vernacular languages. It was thought, therefore, that he would be a natural ally of the Reformers with their appeal to biblical authority. Indeed, Erasmus at first lent his support to Luther, but he soon withdrew it when he saw where the reform movement was leading. He complained, "If only Luther had followed my advice.... I shall not become mixed up in this tragic affair."[2]

Erasmus sought reform in life and practice but not in doctrine. To side openly with Luther, he feared, would be to antagonize the papacy, which still wielded considerable political power. Luther also wished for unity but not at the expense of truth. While Erasmus was willing to underplay doctrinal differences so long as there could be a general moral consensus, Luther was uncompromising over what he considered to be essential doctrines. In a letter to his friend Spalatin (Sept. 9, 1521), Luther remarked that Erasmus was intent not on upholding the cross but only on maintaining peace.

Erasmus finally spoke up against the Reformation in a tract on free will in which he defended the human capacity to come to and respond to the gospel. Luther's answer was his *Bondage of the Will* in which he vigorously reaffirmed the historically evangelical view that apart from Christ man is unable to help himself, that not only faith but the very condition to receive faith is a gift from God. For Erasmus, though sin has weakened man, it has not made him utterly incapable of meritorious action. Erasmus sought to reconcile the biblical teaching about grace and salvation with the classical philosophical belief in human freedom. Luther argued that there can be no compromise between those who elevate human power and those who give all the glory to God in the procuring of human salvation. We are saved, he believed, not by grace working in cooperation with the human will but by grace alone (*sola gratia*), which results in the liberation of the human will from its bondage to the power of sin and death.

Erasmus manifested the skepticism typical of latitudinarianism: We must never be too confident that we are in the right, because we are finite creatures and only life can show whether we are in communion with the true God. Luther went further than Erasmus in maintaining that man in and of himself is totally unable to know or come to the truth, not only because of his finitude, but even more because of his enslavement to sin. Yet Luther argued that once the light of grace shines on us we can know the will and purpose of God, not exhaustively, but truly. Against Erasmus and the spirit of the Renaissance, he unreservedly declared: "The Holy Spirit is no Sceptic, and the things He has written in our hearts are not doubts or opinions, but assertions—surer and more certain than sense and life itself."[3]

Peter T. Forsyth and the New Theology

In the early twentieth century, Peter T. Forsyth, an English Congregationalist pastor and teacher, heralded an exclusive gospel. After serving several parishes, he was called as principal of Hackney College in Hampstead (1901). In his earlier years he had been quite liberal in his theology, but he came to see that only a religion based on the gospel of transforming grace can overthrow the principalities and powers of the world. He wrote: "I was turned from a Christian to a believer, from a lover of love to an object of grace.

And so, whereas I first thought that what the Churches needed was enlightened instruction and liberal theology, I came to be sure that what they needed was evangelization."[4]

As Forsyth came to his evangelical position, he was standing practically alone. Christian theologians and ministers were everywhere attracted to an immanental form of theology inspired by Hegel and Spinoza. The leader of this so-called New Theology was R. J. Campbell, a man of much personal charm, who at a relatively young age had become pastor of the City Temple in London. Campbell believed that every person is a potential Christ, or rather a manifestation of the eternal Christ, and that God is a creative process within nature. His theology was typically eclectic, drawing from a great variety of sources. Robert McAfee Brown has described it as an "amazing jumble of immanentism, theosophy, neoplatonism and quasi pantheism."[5]

Against the New Theology Forsyth declared that Christianity can endure "not by surrendering itself to the modern mind and modern culture, but rather by a break with it: the condition of a long future both for culture and the soul is the Christianity which antagonizes culture without denying its place."[6] The problem was that "the age, and much of the Church, believes in civilization and is interested in the Gospel, instead of believing in the Gospel and being interested in civilization."[7] Confronted with this secular mentality, he argued: "A Gospel which is not exclusive will never include the world, for it will never master it. No religion will include devotees which does not exclude rivals."[8] Forsyth succeeded in turning a great part of the church away from eclecticism and liberalism to a gospel anchored in divine revelation rather than in human wisdom.

Karl Barth and the German Christians

Not long after the death of Forsyth, another theologian rose to prominence on the European scene—Karl Barth, who had served in the Swiss pastorate before becoming professor of theology at various German universities. Barth entered into dire conflict with the German Christians, that party within the German church that sought to accommodate biblical faith to the emerging ideology of National Socialism. In their attempt to sever Christianity from its Jewish roots, the German Christians went so far as to deny the inspiration and canonicity of the Old Testament. Barth was responsible for drawing up the Barmen Confession, which served as the manifesto of the Confessing Church, that group that chose to remain true to the historic evangelical faith. The first article of the Barmen Confession affirms the uniqueness of God's self-revelation in Jesus Christ in unequivocal terms:

> Jesus Christ, as he is attested for us in Holy Scripture, is the one Word of God which we have to hear and which we have to trust and obey in life and in death.

> We reject the false doctrine, as though the Church could and would have to acknowledge as a source of its proclamation, apart from and besides this one Word of God, still other events and powers, figures and truths, as God's revelation.[9]

Barth was severely reprimanded by leading theologians in the state churches of Germany for betraying the church's confessional heritage or at least calling into question its sufficiency. In answer to his critics, Barth insisted that the Barmen Confession stood in continuity with the confessions of the Reformation. The Lutheran scholar Paul Althaus regretted the omission of any mention of the law of God and of general revelation in the Barmen Confession. Gerhard Kittel, describing himself as a National Socialist theologian, professed his adherence to the Twelve Articles drawn up by a group of Nazi theologians and ministers in Tübingen. Kittel, together with Emanuel Hirsch and other German Christians, perceived in the National Socialist movement a "call of God" and expressed gratitude that God had given to the people a leader and deliverer such as Adolf Hitler. Barth rightly saw in the fascination with natural theology the doorway by which the church might appeal to other revelations than the one given in Jesus Christ. Instead of cooperating with the Nazi regime, Barth led the resistance movement against Hitler. In defiance of the edict that required university professors to open their classes with the "Heil Hitler" salute, he courageously opened his classes with prayer. His action was regarded as seditious. Barth was finally debarred from teaching and forced into exile in his native Switzerland.

The Church in a Pluralistic Society

Today it is fashionable to uphold pluralism in the church, but this more often than not betrays a capitulation of the church to cultural ideology. A global perspective, which is prepared to borrow from the religions of the world, is championed over a catholic vision, which strives to bring the whole world under the dominion of Christ. Missions are reappraised to mean the self-development of peoples rather than their conversion. Dialog is stressed over proclamation, the quest for truth over witness to the truth.

While there can and should be a pluralism in witness, there can be no pluralism in doctrine in the holy catholic church. There is room for liturgical diversity, and even for differences of opinion on marginal matters in theology, but there can be no place for a cleavage of thought on the doctrine handed down by the apostles. A church that is both eclectic and catholic cannot long endure, since it means that the household of God is divided against itself.

Christian faith affirms against syncretistic mysticism that God has revealed himself fully and decisively in Jesus Christ, as attested in the Holy Scriptures. It is not the universal mystical awareness of God that is the basis for faith, but the definitive revelation of God in the sacred history mirrored in the Bible. This does not mean that God has left himself without a witness in the world at large (Acts 14:17). His presence is indeed manifested everywhere—in nature and in conscience. Yet Scripture tells us that this general revelation does not bring us saving or true knowledge of God because of the distortion caused by human sin (Rom. 1:18-32). This general knowledge does not prepare the way for the special revelation in Christ but instead renders us inexcusable.

Evangelical Christianity is both exclusive and inclusive. It heralds only one way to salvation, but at the same time it seeks to include the whole world in the saving plan of God. It does not deny that there are partial truths in human philosophy and religion, but it does deny that these truths can deliver men and women from their bondage to sin and death. It does not condemn to hell those people who through circumstances of life have not been exposed to the saving message of reconciliation and redemption through Christ, but it does recognize that such people are spiritually lost and need to be brought into the light of the kingdom. Nor does evangelical Christianity deny that God's redemptive grace may be at work among people of other religions who have access to the Bible or who have heard the good news of Christ second hand (I am thinking here especially of Jews and Moslems who share the prophetic heritage of biblical religion). Evangelical theology does not even discount the possibility that angels from heaven may carry the gospel directly to peoples who grope in the dark and who may never hear the gospel from the lips of a missionary. It does reject the now commonly held view that pagans who live up to the light within them might be considered anonymous Christians or that all peoples whether they believe or not are already in the kingdom of Christ.

Evangelical faith seeks to bring the faint reflections of truth in various religious traditions and philosophies into the service of the gospel. Just as pagans can be baptized and sanctified by the Spirit of truth, so pagan thoughtforms can be baptized by this same Spirit into the service of truth. Religious eclecticism, on the other hand, tries to combine the insights of non-Christian systems of thought with those of the Christian faith in order to reach a higher synthesis, which is tantamount to a new religion. In the former instance, non-Christian insights are purified and transformed in the light of the searing judgment of the gospel; in the latter, these insights are appropriated apart from the critical discernment of an exclusivistic faith.

Catholicism vs. Eclecticism

The true church is characterized not by eclecticism or syncretism but by catholicity. It is not a mystical fraternity or religious society but the body of Christ. It is united not on the basis of a common religious experience but on the basis of a divine revelation given once for all in the history of Jesus Christ (Heb. 10). Against eclectic religiosity, the church affirms the holy catholic faith, which excludes and negates before it includes and fulfills.

Catholicism and eclecticism indeed signify two different religions.[10] Whereas eclecticism contends that all roads lead to God, catholicism holds that the only road that leads to God is the road by which God comes to man—Jesus Christ. Catholicism is ready to acknowledge that other roads are not utterly bereft of the light of God, but it insists that this light is sufficient only for our condemnation, not for our salvation. While eclecticism presupposes that all truths can be harmonized, catholicism is emphatic that partial truths need to be corrected and fulfilled in the perspective of the ultimate truth embodied in Jesus Christ. Eclecticism understands revelation in terms of insight into the mystery of life, which is common to all religion. Catholicism sees revelation as a divine intervention into the history of a particular people, which calls into question all human religion. Eclecticism is inclined to accept the view that supernatural truth builds on natural truth. Catholicism avers that supernatural truth purifies and transforms natural truth. Eclecticism sees the goal of religion as the discovery of Christ already present in all peoples. Catholicism understands the goal of religion as bringing the whole world under the lordship of Christ. Both orientations uphold reconciliation, but while eclecticism speaks of the reconciliation of disparate philosophies, catholicism strives for the reconciliation of all peoples under Christ.

We must contend for the truth, but in the spirit of love. We ought not regard the lost peoples of the world as living under the curse of a predestination to damnation but rather as objects of God's love. They too are born under the sign of the cross, for Christ died for the world as well as for the church. We may regard all peoples with hope, knowing that the grace of our Lord Jesus Christ is able to save to the uttermost, that the love of Christ goes out to the whole creation. Our mission is not to save a select few, but to bring all peoples into the kingdom of Christ.

I do not seek virtues
but the Lord of virtues.
Teresa of Avila

A true Christian conquers
when he is conquered.
Stephen prevailed
over his enemies
when they seemed
to prevail over him.
Richard Sibbes

One must reach the point
of 'not caring two straws
about his own status'
before he can wish wholly
for God's Kingdom, not
his own, to be established.
C. S. Lewis

7
Heroism

HOW OFTEN AT SPIRITUAL life or "higher life" conferences, people are challenged to do something great for God! They are summoned to acts of daring and valor that sometimes make the deeds of cultural heroes pale into insignificance. Yet is this the meaning of discipleship under the cross?

Heroism is indeed to be included among the misunderstandings of what constitutes true religion. This is a danger that is often overlooked because Christians do seem to be called to a certain degree of heroism. We are urged to become saints (1 Cor. 1:2), to strive for the holiness without which no one will see the Lord (Heb. 12:14). The Christian life is one of costly obedience. Yet we are not called to "greatness" as the tradition of heroism understands it. Sanctity involves disciplining the flesh and overcoming temptation, but it is far from the triumphalism commonly associated with heroism, including religious heroism.

Hellenistic Heroes and Biblical Saints

In Greek popular religion, heroes were individuals of courage and wisdom who had been elevated to the status of demigods. Being more than men but less than gods, they supposedly could intercede with the gods on behalf of mortals. Heroism was closely associated with greatness or nobility of spirit. Greatness meant transcending the ordinary by aiming for the highest, even at considerable risk. In defying malignant power, heroes exceeded human expectations. They were therefore believed to possess something superior to human virtue.

Heroism was also related to tragedy in classical culture. The truly great man would inevitably become a tragic hero: in seeking the highest he would forget that he was only a creature and thereby suffer retribution or nemesis. The tragic flaw was hubris—a kind of prideful insolence that posed a challenge to the gods; it is not to be confused with an idolatrous pride that seeks to displace the gods (or the supreme power). Hubris is best understood as unwise self-elevation, transgressing the limits assigned by the gods or fate. It proceeded from the vitalities of nature, not from a corrupted heart. Behind hubris lay ignorance: the hero, whose vision was limited by his finitude, invariably failed to grasp the gravity of the situation in which he found himself. Finally he began to understand but only when it was too late. This is why it can be said that the salient mark of the tragic is the state of being blind.

There is always an element of self-pity in the tragic hero. He needs a chorus to extol his virtues and justify his actions. The tragic hero is not responsible for his plight, because he is a victim of blindness and ignorance. It is bad judgment and the circumstances of life that have brought about his downfall. He is punished not for unwarranted exaltation of self but for authentic greatness. The proper attitude toward the hero is a mixture of pity and admiration.

In the early church Christian theologians tried to reconcile the Greek ideal of heroism and the biblical ideal of sainthood. The martyrs and confessors of the faith became the new heroes. Asceticism came to be seen as an unmistakable sign of heroism, since it represented the conquest of self. Just as the heroes of Greek and Roman mythology battled with gods and dragons, Christian heroes wrestled with demons.

Yet something was lost in the synthesis of these two ideals. A false notion of sainthood entered the church when it accommodated to the cult of the hero. A saint became one who challenged and triumphed over the powers of darkness rather than a humble recipient of divine grace. Extraordinary feats of asceticism were prized over ordinary acts of loving-kindness and mercy. True religion was imagined to be a higher order of life involving voluntary poverty and renunciation of marriage. Sanctity was envisioned as a ladder to be climbed only by divesting oneself of all earthly attachments. The church taught that with the assistance of grace one could finally gain heroic virtue, a moral excellence that merited both human praise and divine favor.

In general, the Reformation disputed any correlation between sainthood and heroism. The Renaissance and Enlightenment, however, were receptive to the classical ideal, though an optimistic view of the heroic life came to prevail over the tragic outlook of classicism. In the liberal theology flowing out of the Enlightenment, the heroic ideal was reinterpreted as gaining mastery over nature or becoming a determiner of history. Human beings were no longer impotent in the face of destiny but could now fashion their own destiny. In the Social Gospel movement, the hero was an enlightened social reformer, a person of courage and valor who strove to overthrow the bastions of oppression in society. Today liberation theology seeks to recover this heroic dimension of religion; social revolutionaries like Che Guevara and Camilo Torres are in effect the new saints.

When the ideal of heroism intrudes into Christian faith, the picture of Christ is invariably and adversely altered. Jesus becomes a prophetic figure who towers above the prejudices and taboos of his age, a sagacious leader who defies the oppressive structures in religion and society. In the devotional literature at the beginning of this century, Jesus was often depicted as "a mighty, glorious man," a commanding personality, "tempted like ourselves, but victorious."[1]

True religion calls us to take up the cross and follow Christ, but it does not promise the kind of victory over the evils of the world that the world expects. The badge of the Christian is suffering, not conquest. The church is not to be confused with a power structure that seeks to impose its will on society. Instead it is what Luther called "the little flock of the faint-hearted" who live by the grace and mercy of God. The strong will not ultimately conquer the world. Rather the meek will inherit it (Mt. 5:5). Meekness, not self-assertiveness, distinguishes the saint. Not to be confused with weakness, meekness is a holy defenselessness that proves more powerful than the powers of the world. It might be defined as the strength to love. Jesus sent out his disciples as "sheep among wolves" (Mt. 10:16 NIV); his sheep rely for their survival on their Shepherd, not on their own resources.

A Qualitative Difference

Despite some outward similarities, sanctity is qualitatively distinct from heroism. Sanctity means nearness to God; heroism means defiance of fate. Sanctity is love of the unlovable; heroism is love of the ideal. Heroism aspires to heights bordering on the divine; sanctity means surrender to the divine. Heroes have fame; saints have infamy. Heroism exalts what is noble over what is vulgar; sanctity upholds what is loving over what is hardhearted. Heroism regards humility with suspicion, but humility is the very essence of sanctity. The opposite of heroism is cowardice or timidity; the opposite of sanctity is prayerlessness.

Saints do not suffer misfortune or tragedy (as a hero does) but persecution, even martyrdom. Their martyrdom, moreover, stems not from some tragic flaw (as does the hero's suffering), but from opposition to their message. Saints rejoice in their sufferings (Rom. 5:3; Col. 1:24) whereas suffering heroes appeal to the sympathy of others. A Catholic priest, Father Kentenich, who was imprisoned in Dachau for four years during World War 2, testified: "Dachau was not hell for us, but rather heaven. How often we said that to each other then! For what is heaven but the deep fellowship of love with the Triune God and with those who love him." Richard Wurmbrand, a Lutheran pastor who spent fourteen years in a Communist prison in his native Rumania, could write: "Alone in my cell, cold, hungry and in rags, I danced for joy every night."[2]

The world can admire heroism, but its attitude toward persons such as the two prisoners above is apt to be one of bewilderment or suspicion (Is. 59:15; Hos. 9:7; Mk. 3:21; Jn. 10:20; Acts 26:24). The saint, unlike the hero, does not seek tears of pity from others but tears of repentance (Lk. 23:28). That is why the world is drawn to heroes but cannot tolerate saints.

Sanctity may actually entail the sacrifice of greatness—a flight from heroism—should love so demand. A disciple must be willing to follow Christ into obscurity. The nineteenth-century French Carmelite nun Thérèse of Lisieux upheld the "little way" over the "heroic way." She refused to discuss her virtues, acknowledging that in the sight of God she was still a sinner. Instead of a ladder to heaven, she preferred to speak of a "lift" or "elevator" to heaven, the lift of free grace.

A Christian is not intent on world mastery or creative self-affirmation. The progress of a saint, as Gerald Heard puts it, is measured by a "blessed corrosion" that eats away the wish for one's own way, one's own ideals and one's own hopes. The lives of saints may contain tragic or heroic elements, but they will never be tragic heroes. Their acts spring not from heroic qualities but from the folly of suffering love. Their suffering always points beyond tragedy to the redemption of the world in Christ.

Saints are powerful in their weakness, that is, in the confession of their helplessness apart from God. When we cling to God in our weakness, we find in God the source of our strength. The power of God, said Paul, is made perfect in our weakness, in humble dependence on his grace and mercy (2 Cor. 12:9; cf. 1 Cor. 1:25). J. Hudson Taylor observed, "All God's giants have been weak men who did great things for God because they reckoned on God being with them."

Christians will have both virtues and vices. Yet we need to repent of our virtues as well as our vices, because the two are always mixed together. As Christians we will confess with Isaiah that in the sight of God "all our righteous acts are like filthy rags" (Is. 64:6 NIV). Hence we will depend for our salvation not on our own spirituality, ascetic disciplines, or works of charity, but on Christ's perfect righteousness, which is received by faith alone.

The examples of sanctity given in the Bible do not conform to what the wisdom of the world judges as heroism. Abraham's willingness to sacrifice his son Isaac is regarded by the world as religious fanaticism, not heroism. Gideon's marching with three hundred men armed only with trumpets and pitchers against tens of thousands of Midianites appears to be an act of folly and naiveté, certainly not of heroic courage. Moses, Elijah, Jonah and Jeremiah were men pursued by God; by no means did they seek to ascend to heights of either worldly or spiritual glory. They were made bold to witness for God, but often against their own inclinations. Daniel did not do battle with the lions in their den but instead quietly "trusted in his God" (Dan. 6:23).

Neither Jesus nor Paul was a hero in the popular sense. The Bible shows that both were ready to flee from those who wished to kill them. Jesus accepted death reluctantly. Death is evil in the eyes of Christians (Rom. 6:23; 1 Cor. 15:54-56). Greek philosophers, by contrast, held death was good. "What can be greater," Socrates asked, "than to be with the sons of God? Be of good cheer about death."

The early Christian martyrs marched into the flames of fire prepared for them, singing hymns and blessing their captors. Their deaths were tragic only for their tormentors, who had to reap the consequences of such crimes. In the third century St. Lawrence, having suffered in flames on an iron bed for some time, turned to his captors and said with a cheerful smile, "Let my body be turned, one side is broiled enough." Sanctity is closer to what the world deems foolhardiness than to the bravery of heroes. Many of the saints did possess such natural virtues as courage, temperance and fortitude, but these were not what made them saints.

In the seventeenth century George Fox, founder of the Quakers, preached in the open air in the face of adversaries intent on his destruction. After being struck in the face for telling people to be humane, he would wipe away the blood and finish what he had to say. On one occasion he was knocked down, kicked and trampled until he fainted. Regaining consciousness, he said to the crowd's amazement, "Strike again; here are my arms, my head, and my cheeks." Fox demonstrated both holy boldness and meekness, which is not passivity but the "violence of love" that challenges the powers of evil through a readiness for martyrdom.

In the following century, John Wesley was frequently hounded by mobs, but never lost his self-composure. Once he was stoned and then dragged into an alley and left for dead. Yet he could return from such an incident to stand in the midst of his detractors to preach the Word of God. Wesley never reproached or denounced his persecutors. He overcame the world not through stubbornness or valor but through faith—absolute dependence on God.

C. T. Studd

Early in this century we have the example of C. T. Studd, founder of the Heart of Africa Mission, later renamed the Worldwide Evangelization Crusade. Coming from a wealthy family and educated at Eton and Cambridge, he was converted in one of Dwight L. Moody's evangelistic campaigns in England. After serving as a missionary in China and India, at the age of fifty-two Studd felt called by God to carry the gospel into the African interior. In fragile health, warned by his doctor not to make the journey, almost penniless (having given away his inheritance), he set out for the Sudan in complete submission to God. His wife, who later became an invalid, tried to dissuade him (as did his closest friends), but to no avail. He returned to England only once, and after his second departure for Africa (this time the Belgian Congo) in 1916, he saw his wife for only a single fortnight of the remaining fifteen years of his life.[3]

The rigors of the jungle proved to be almost too much for this redoubtable warrior of God. Among his afflictions were asthma, recurring malaria and dysentery and the chills and pains of gallstones. He confessed: "Sometimes I feel... that my cross is heavy beyond endurance, and I fear I often feel like fainting under it, but I hope to go on and not faint."[4] Funds and recruits came to him by prayer alone. Yet despite great hardship, his missionary efforts bore amazing fruit. Eventually the work expanded rapidly into other countries besides the Congo.

A hero is inclined to prepare for battle by making reasonably sure he has the resources to overcome and persevere. By contrast, C. T. Studd ventured forth in sheer faith, heeding only God's command and trusting only in God's promises. He counted the cost, but he was willing to pay the price, even if it meant his death (Lk. 14:28).

The incontrovertible gulf between authentic sanctity and classical heroism is illustrated by C. T. Studd's reaction to fears of what would happen to the Heart of Africa Mission if he should die: "We will all shout Hallelujah! The world will have lost its biggest fool, and with one fool less to handicap him, God will do greater wonders still. There shall be no funeral, no wreaths, crape, nor tears.... Our God will still be alive and nothing else matters."[5]

The only claim to worldly fame of that humble laborer in the kingdom was that he had been a cricket champion at Cambridge. God often accomplishes his purposes through the weak and ailing—through the weak and *obedient*, that is, not the strong and *disobedient*. C. T. Studd was not pursuing recognition or glory. He was intent only on following the divine imperative.

We have a more contemporary example in Paul Schneider, the "pastor of Buchenwald." For preaching that Jesus, not Hitler, is Lord, Schneider, a minister in the German Reformed church, was incarcerated in the notorious prison at Buchenwald. Placed in solitary confinement for refusing to salute the Nazi flag, he eventually died from the effects of torture. Had he signed a small piece of paper promising to give up the care of his church, Schneider would have been allowed to go free. Yet even in his prison cell he would not keep quiet; his voice could be heard shouting words of comfort to his fellow prisoners and words of judgment on his tormentors, calling the Nazi guards to repentance. He stood firm for the truth, not to gain fame or insure his reputation, but out of concern for his fellow prisoners and for his oppressors. His witness was made out of love, not out of defiance.

Works of Faith

The works of faith associated with the saints are best understood as fruits or manifestations of the Spirit, not as acts of virtue as such. Though they are indeed human acts, they derive not from natural strength or power but from the infusion of grace. Saints are used by God in a mighty way, but they are aware that in themselves they are only frail reeds. Heroes, on the other hand, conscious of their innate strength and powers, seek to realize a vocation to greatness. Heroes are willing to give up their lives for the sake of a lofty principle whereas saints are willing to sacrifice both life and principles for the poor and downtrodden of the world.

It is possible to speak of a Christian heroism in a qualified sense, but this contradicts what the world, even the religious world, understands by heroism. Throughout history, mystics and sages have commonly regarded sanctity as a mountain to be scaled, and self-knowledge and self-discipline as the means of ascent. For biblical Christians, on the contrary, sanctity is a descent from the mountain of rapturous experience into the valley of lowly service. Discipleship under the cross may well entail venture and risk, but it is not the same as heroic asceticism or the idealistic heroism associated with social reform and revolution. These things may be good on their own level, but they are not the same as sanctity or holiness in the Christian sense.

We are summoned to work out our own salvation "with fear and trembling" (Phil. 2:12), to "strive ... for the holiness without which no one will see the Lord" (Heb. 12:14-15; cf. Mt. 5:48). Yet our striving is made possible only through the grace of God who works in us, "inspiring both the will and the deed, for his own chosen purpose" (Phil. 2:13 NEB). We are conquerors only because nothing "will be able to separate us from the love of God that is in Christ Jesus our Lord" (Rom. 8:39 NIV). We are conquerors, moreover, even in the midst of defeat and humiliation in the eyes of the world. If we take up the cross and follow Christ, we are promised the crown of salvation (1 Cor. 9:24-25; 2 Tim. 4:8; 1 Pet. 5:4). Yet this crown is, in the last analysis, a free gift of God assured to us not apart from our striving, but also not as a reward for our striving.

P. T. Forsyth underlines the contrast between true religion and spiritual heroism: "Christianity is not the sacrifice we make, but the sacrifice we trust; not the victory we win, but the victory we inherit. That is the evangelical principle."[6]

Dietrich Bonhoeffer, too, saw the gulf between evangelical Christianity and the perennial fascination with heroism: "The quest for the superman, the endeavour to outgrow the man within the man, the pursuit of the heroic, the cult of the demigod, all this is not the proper concern of man. . . . The real man is not an object either for contempt or for deification, but an object of the love of God."[7]

The prototype of the hero is the mythological figure Prometheus, who was not a mortal but a titan or demigod. Prometheus courageously stole fire from the celestial hearth as a gift for humanity. Because of his audacity and defiance, he was chained to a mountain peak where an eagle tore out his liver by day and it grew again by night.

The prototype of the saint is Jesus, who was noted not for defiance of God but for his godly fear. Whereas Prometheus tried to transcend his limitations, Christ entered into our limitations. He was exalted in his humiliation. Unlike the punishment that Prometheus suffered, the crucifixion of Christ was not a tragedy but the resolution of tragedy.

The death of Christ was the outcome not of heroic self-affirmation but of the obedience of faith. Moreover, Christ died not just as a martyr but as a Savior. He was killed because of who he was, not simply because of his message. There is only one death for sin, though there will always be many deaths for the sake of faith.

We are called to present our bodies as "living sacrifices" (Rom. 12:1), not in order to gain merit before God nor to win the praise of others nor even to express ourselves as free beings. The motivation for "bearing the cross" is to witness to the cross of Jesus Christ. Our deeds and words should call attention not to our own accomplishments or experiences but to his great work, which alone atones for the sins of the world. Our focus should be not on ourselves —on our strengths or deficiencies—but on the sufficiency of the cross of Christ.

Bonhoeffer in his prison cell could not get away from Jeremiah 45:5: "Seekest thou great things for thyself? Seek them not" (KJV). We should not be preoccupied with things too grand for us (Ps. 131:1-2). Yet we should be willing to do even greater things out of fidelity to our Lord who directs us to stand against the stream, who summons us to do battle with the powers of darkness, who calls us to win victories in his name and for his sake, but victories that sometimes appear to be crushing defeats in the eyes of the world.

The paradox is that in being servants of Christ we become masters of the world, but in seeking to be masters of the world we become subject to the powers of the world (Mt. 16:24-26; Lk. 9:23-27). By carrying the cross, we gain the crown; by humbling ourselves, we are exalted; by descending into the depths of the world's despair, we ascend to the heights of the paradise that God prepares for those who love him. At the same time, we should always remember that it is only by grace that we can identify with the world's afflictions. Therefore we can take pride as little in our self-renunciation as in our heroic self-affirmation. But we can be forever grateful to God who in his infinite mercy chose us and called us to our holy vocation.

Christianity introduces a transvaluation of values. We now recognize that most of what the world esteems is nothing but vanity and deceit. On the other hand, values the world is prone to reject are now seen as the key to new life and a renewed world. It is the poor in spirit who will enter the kingdom of God, the meek who will inherit the earth, the pure in heart who will see God, those who hunger and thirst not for riches or fame but for righteousness who will be satisfied (Mt. 5). The blessed are not those who are esteemed by the world, but those who are hated and excluded by the world because of the Son of Man (Lk. 6:22, 26).

An age that upholds the ideal of heroism is preferable

to an age fascinated by antiheroes. Better an emphasis on human virtue than on human weakness. Still better is an age that sounds the call to sainthood, that summons us out of ourselves, out of our hopes and fears, out of our dreams and disappointments, into the service of the kingdom of God.

The story of the Church
is the story of many
resurrections.
John Calvin

A grain of living faith
is worth more than
a pound of historic
knowledge; and a drop of
love, than an ocean
of science.
*Count Nicolaus Ludwig
von Zinzendorf*

There is no use
talking about love
if it does not relate
to the stuff of life
in the area of material
possessions and needs.
If it does not mean
a sharing of our material
things for our brothers
in Christ close at home
and abroad, it means
little or nothing.
Francis Schaeffer

8
Toward the Recovery of True Religion

WE NEED TODAY TO BE reminded that the kingdom of God does not consist in food or drink or in any outward rituals or observances but in righteousness, peace and joy in the Holy Spirit. This kingdom, moreover, is a gift of God, not a human accomplishment. Its foundation is the vicarious atonement of Jesus Christ on Calvary. It was carried forward by the great outpouring of the Holy Spirit at Pentecost.

The disciples before that day of Pentecost were only disciples. They tried to follow Jesus and his teachings as best they could, but they still did not know true religion. It was only at Pentecost that they were truly made apostles. Then they experienced the power of the resurrection of Jesus Christ. Then they were emboldened by the Holy

Spirit to bear witness to Christ publicly. Whereas previously they were disciples of the One whom they saw as the Messiah of Israel, now they were ambassadors and heralds of the risen Christ. Instead of a seeking faith that is a dead work of the law, they now had the faith that empowers and redeems. Before they had the faith of servants; now they had the faith of sons. Before they were plagued by timidity and fearfulness; now they were ready to die for the sake of their Master and Savior.

Being before Doing

Faith includes intellectual assent, but its essence is a personal relationship with Jesus Christ. It consists basically in a living union with Jesus through the Holy Spirit. True faith means *being* before *doing*—being in the favor of God before doing the will of God. It means being grasped by the Spirit of God. It is an opening of our inward eyes to the reality of God's incomparable love poured out for sinners in the sacrificial life and death of Jesus Christ.

Yet faith is not only a mighty action of the Holy Spirit on the soul but also our action in the power of the Spirit as we are sent forth into the world as witnesses and ambassadors of Christ. Faith entails both radical passivity and radical activity. As Luther observed: "Faith... is a living, busy, active, mighty thing... so it is impossible for it not to do good works incessantly."[1]

The bane of many churches today is an empty formalism or a barren biblicism, either of which degenerates into an oppressive legalism. Other churches that seem more vital are plagued by a perfectionistic enthusiasm or a frenetic activism that borders on humanism. What is needed is a recovery of the depth and breadth of apostolic faith, a revival of true religion. It is important to bear in mind that Jesus Christ is not just a moral ideal or a prophetic genius but a living Savior. He is not simply the human representative of God but God himself in human flesh. It is not enough to know the historical facts about the life of Christ, how he lived and died. Each person must know that Jesus died for him or her personally.

John Wesley before his Aldersgate experience was a model of moral rectitude. He fasted, prayed and preached, yet his soul was in a state of constant unrest. He had been baptized, confirmed and ordained; yet he still did not have faith effectual for salvation. His religion consisted in earnestly striving to keep the commandments; it was devoid of the assurance of salvation that comes from relying on Christ's righteousness and not our own.

Then one evening Wesley heard Martin Luther's *Preface to the Epistle to the Romans* being read at a prayer meeting on Aldersgate Street in London. He confessed that his heart was "strangely warmed." In his words: "I felt I did trust in Christ, Christ alone for salvation, and an assurance was given me that he had taken away *my* sins, even *mine*, and saved *me* from the law of sin and death."[2] Before that decisive turning point in his life, he described himself as "almost a Christian." Not until then did he come to know the joy and peace of our Lord Jesus Christ.

Wesley then embarked on a campaign of itinerant evangelism to bring the saving message of God's free grace to the middle class and working people of England. Some scholars contend that England was thus saved from the kind of violent revolution that brought down the monarchy in France. The revolution that Wesley preached was a moral one, planting the seeds for widespread social and economic reforms, some of which sprouted and bore fruit that same century.

Wesley, Tauler, Pascal and countless other men and women who have experienced the breakthrough into freedom bear witness that the Holy Spirit is not a concept but a living reality. Many liturgical churches repeat Sunday after Sunday the words of the Apostles' Creed: "I believe in the Holy Ghost," often a helpful exercise. Yet many people in our churches have no first-hand acquaintance with the Holy Spirit. We are still in the prison of fear until we begin to know the love, peace and joy that come to us through the baptism of the Holy Spirit (Rom. 5:5; 15:13).

True religion does not consist in imposing our views on others but in sharing the light that has been given to us. In our evangelistic task we do not approach others with any pretension to greater virtue or intellectual acumen. Instead, we present ourselves as fellow sinners whose eyes have been opened both to the gravity of the human predicament and to the reality of God's unconditional grace and love. The word that we proclaim stands in judgment over our lives as well as the lives of our hearers. We are beggars telling others where they can get food. As "fishers of men" we are instrumental in advancing the kingdom of God, but it is not through our cleverness that people are won to Jesus Christ; our task is simply to let down the net of the gospel. As the vehicle of the Spirit, the gospel itself brings in souls for the kingdom (Lk. 5:2-10).

This is not to imply that Christians should never use apologetic arguments in defense of the faith. But our purpose in doing so is not to induce a decision of faith (only the Spirit does that through the preaching of the Word). Rather our aim is to intensify the hunger for faith in the human soul and to help those who already believe to understand their faith better. We can show the intellectual relevance of our faith by argumentation. But faith's concrete relevance to the human condition can be grasped only by those whose minds have been touched by the illumination of the Holy Spirit.

Our witness is not to peak experiences of the sacred, but to the incursion of the sacred into the secular which we see in Jesus Christ. Our appeal is not to external evidences for the faith but to evidences that faith itself provides: the empty tomb, the transformed lives of the disciples, the interior witness of the Holy Spirit. In carrying out the evangelistic mandate, we must bear in mind that Holy Scripture is its own best interpreter, that is to say, Scripture illumined by the Spirit. Holy Scripture in the hands of Spirit-directed believers is sufficient to "demolish arguments and every pretension that sets itself up against the knowledge of God" (2 Cor. 10:5 NIV).

We should never confuse true religion with techniques for cultivating spirituality or programs of church growth. It is God who gives the increase, though it is up to us to plant the seed (1 Cor. 3:6-7). Our responsibility is to hear the Word and then share the good news. We can serve the kingdom of God, but we cannot build it. The kingdom is a gift from God that can only be received with gratefulness.

The Sword of the Spirit
True religion is characterized by a deep and abiding respect for Holy Scripture as the Word of God. It will lead to diligent Bible study and to a frequent use of the Bible in personal devotions. Yet the goal of the revelation that comes to us in Scripture is not right understanding as such, but life in communion with Christ. The intent of revelation is fulfilled not simply in the perception of the cross but in obedience under the cross. The truth in the Bible must take effect in the life history of the reader and hearer if it is to result in salvation. The events of redemption described in the Bible must be reenacted in the interior life of the believer if the Bible is to realize its role as a lamp to our feet and a light for our path (Ps. 119:105).

The Word of God, to be sure, is an objective reality that meets us in the Scriptures, in the sermon and in the sacrament. Yet this Word from God is not intended to remain something external to us. As the sword of the Spirit, it breaks into the inner recesses of our being (2 Cor. 4:4-6; Col. 3:16; 2 Pet. 1:19). The temple of God is not a building made by human hands but God's dwelling place in the soul of the believer (1 Cor. 3:16-17; 6:19; Eph. 2:21-22). Once the Word of God enters our inner being, it compels us to reorder our lives and to proclaim the hope it offers to all the world. The prophet Jeremiah described the Word of God as a "burning fire shut up in my bones" (Jer. 20:9). We do not really know God's Word simply by learning propositional truth: This truth must take root within us as a purging and cleansing force for righteousness (Ps. 51:6-7; Prov. 2:1-10; Col. 3:15-16; 1 Jn. 2:14).

Profoundly aware of our constant need for the resources of God's grace, we will hold the office of preaching in high esteem. Yet we dare not make a simple equation between the words of the preacher and the Word of God. We should try to hear the heavenly word of Christ in and through the earthly word of his ambassador. At the same time, we must judge all human words in the light of the Word given to us in the Bible.

While the preaching of the gospel can indeed be an effectual means of grace (Rom. 10:17; 1 Cor. 1:21; 2 Cor. 5:20; Titus 1:3; Rev. 12:11), we should always keep in mind that God may withhold his Word from his servants because of unconfessed personal or social sin. Or God may withdraw his presence in order to test and discipline his people. Those who preach need always to pray with the psalmist: "Take not the word of truth utterly out of my mouth; for I have hoped in thy judgments" (Ps. 119:43 KJV). Even with many preachers in the land, there may still be a famine of the Word of God (Amos 8:11-12; Jer. 5:30-31). On the other hand, a preacher who bears testimony to Christ brokenly but in prayerful dependence on him can still be used as an instrument of God's Spirit in winning souls for the kingdom. Even when the preacher is giving a sound and admirable exposition of scriptural truth, the Spirit may be speaking a Word different from the word the preacher intends. Moreover, the Spirit may occasionally speak over and above and sometimes even against the preacher's own witness so that people can still hear and believe.

Whether it comes to us in Scripture or the sermon, the Word of God is never a general truth that can be summarily received or dismissed. It is always a concrete word addressed to people in their historical particularity. It demands not simply the assent of our minds but the obedience of our wills. It is apprehended only by those who sense their inadequacy and helplessness. It is disclosed specifically to those who humble themselves before God and earnestly seek his mercy and guidance. Only those "who tremble at his word" hear his Word (Is. 66:2, 5; Ps. 119: 161-162 NIV). Only those who acknowledge their sin and cry to God for his forgiveness come to know God's will and purpose for their lives. Yet we could not humble ourselves apart from the motivating power of faith. We could not seek unless we were already found by his grace.

God's Word is not simply available to human conception or perception. It may, by the miracle of divine grace, be conveyed through the Bible and the proclamation of the church, but at the same time it is hidden in these human forms of witness. God's Word can be known only through God's Spirit.

True religion makes a place for sacraments, but disclaims sacramentalism. Grace is not automatically dispensed by the mere performance of certain rites. God cannot be encased in a sacramental box. He is free to withhold himself in the sacraments as well as to reveal himself. The sacraments can never be a substitute for the Word, written and proclaimed, but must always be subordinate to the Word. At the same time, biblical religion acknowledges baptism and the Lord's Supper as genuine means of grace by which God acts to seal the fruits of Christ's redemption in those who believe. The sacraments by themselves cannot communicate the grace of God, but when united with the Word and faith they can be powerful aids in promoting the spiritual life.

The kind of religion I uphold here is concerned with purity in worship, purity in doctrine, purity in life. It is vigorously opposed to doctrinal indifferentism or a false irenicism. Yet its basis lies not in doctrinal or confessional loyalty, nor in ritual purity, but in being united with Jesus Christ by faith. Its essence is personal devotion to Christ. True spirituality means being gripped by the passion of inward commitment to the incarnate Lord.

Personal Experience

There is a difference between believing that Christ is the Savior of humankind in general and coming to know him as one's own Savior. Faith, understood as an interior awakening to the glory and meaning of the cross, is a gift of God. It is a work of the Holy Spirit within us. If we do not have this kind of faith, let us seek it. Let us pray for it. The key to discipleship is given by our Lord: "Ask, and it will be given you; seek, and you will find; knock, and it will be opened to you" (Mt. 7:7).

True religion is inseparable from an experience of the divine holiness and the divine love. Sometimes that experience will take dramatic form, as when the apostle Paul was lifted up into the "third heaven" (2 Cor. 12:2). Yet those who have such experiences do not dwell on them. People of faith are not spiritual exhibitionists, but heralds and ambassadors of Jesus Christ. Living on a "religious high" is not serving the glory of God and advancing his kingdom. John the Baptist furnished the model of true spirituality when he declared, "He must increase, but I must decrease" (Jn. 3:30).

Humility such as this is an indispensable mark of authentic piety. No one can be confronted by the holy God without having a poignant sense of one's own creatureliness and sinfulness (Is. 6:1-5). What shows us the depth of our sin and the magnitude of God's grace is not just an awareness of God as the Holy One, which all people have to some degree, but the knowledge of the holy love of God reflected in the life and death of Jesus Christ. Humility is the key to the love of human beings for God and for one another. Proud people cannot love, because to love means to be emptied of self and dedicated to the glory of God and the welfare of others.

True religion has an ethical as well as a spiritual dimension. It will inevitably issue in both works of piety (prayer, meditation, devotion) and works of mercy. It will strive to give honor to God as well as meet both the spiritual and the legitimate material needs of an ailing and despairing humanity.

The cardinal evidence of true religion is works of self-giving love which are visible to the world (Mt. 7:20; Jn. 13:35; Rom. 14:18; Jas. 1:27). Such works will not be visible, however, to those who do them, for the focus of faithful doers is never on their good deeds (to which they are oblivious) but on Christ and his great work of atonement.

The essence of true religion, the righteousness of faith, is known only to God. True religion will be manifested in fruits, but before we can bear fruit we must be rooted in Christ, engrafted into him. We must be born again from above by the Holy Spirit (cf. Jn. 1:12-13; 3:5-8; 1 Pet. 1:3).

Notes

Chapter 2
[1]Cited in Heinrich Boehmer, *Road to Reformation*, trans. John W. Doberstein and Theodore G. Tappert (Philadelphia: Muhlenberg Press, 1946), pp. 110-11.

Chapter 3
[1]Cited in Francis MacNutt, *The Power to Heal* (Notre Dame, Ind.: Ave Maria Press, 1977), p. 195.
[2]August Hermann Francke, *Werke in Auswahl*, ed. Erhard Peschke (Berlin: Luther-Verlag, 1969), p. 13.
[3]Ibid., pp. 27-28.
[4]In Eberhard Bethge, *Dietrich Bonhoeffer*, trans. Eric Mosbacher (London: Collins, 1970), p. 154.
[5]Cited in Mary Bosanquet, *The Life and Death of Dietrich Bonhoeffer* (New York: Harper & Row, 1968), p. 278.

Chapter 4
[1]"Heidelberg Disputation," *Luther's Works*, Vol. 31, ed. Harold J. Grimm (Philadelphia: Muhlenberg Press, 1957), p. 57.
[2]See Arthur Lovejoy, *The Great Chain of Being* (Cambridge, Mass.: Harvard Univ. Press, 1976), pp. 201-7.
[3]Malcolm Muggeridge, *Something Beautiful for God: Mother Teresa of Calcutta* (New York: Harper & Row, 1971), p. 67.
[4]Ibid., p. 112.
[5]Ibid., p. 66.
[6]Corrie ten Boom, *This Day Is the Lord's* (Old Tappan, N. J.: Fleming H. Revell Co., 1979), p. 174.

Chapter 5
[1]John K. Ryan, ed. and trans., *The Confessions of St. Augustine* (Garden City, N.Y.: Doubleday Image Books, 1960), Bk. 10, Chap. 32, p. 260.
[2]Ibid., Bk. 10, Chap. 35, p. 265.
[3]Martin Luther, *Treatise on Good Works* (1520) in *Works of Martin Luther*, Vol. 1, trans. W. A. Lambert (Philadelphia: A. J. Holman Co., 1915), p. 192.
[4]In T. H. L. Parker, *Portrait of Calvin* (Philadelphia: Westminster Press, 1961), p.64.
[5]Ibid., p. 65.

[6]In John T. McNeill, *The History and Character of Calvinism*, rpt. (New York: Oxford Univ. Press, 1977), p. 230.

[7]*The Complete Works of Saint Teresa of Jesus*, ed. E. Allison Peers, Vol. I (New York: Sheed & Ward, 1946), p. 141.

[8]Stephen Clissold, ed., *The Wisdom of the Spanish Mystics* (New York: New Direction Books, 1980), p. 76.

[9]Cf. 1 Thess. 5:12-13; Heb. 13:17; 1 Pet. 5:5.

Chapter 6

[1]See William A. Clebsch's preface in *Athanasius–The Life of Antony and the Letter to Marcellinus*, trans. Robert C. Gregg (New York: Paulist Press, 1980), pp. xiii–xxi.

[2]Martin Luther, *The Bondage of the Will*, trans. and introd. J. I. Packer and O. R. Johnston (Old Tappan, N.J.: Fleming H. Revell Co., 1957), p. 31.

[3]Ibid., p. 70.

[4]P. T. Forsyth, *Positive Preaching and the Modern Mind* (London: Independent Press Ltd., Fourth Impression, 1953), p. 193.

[5]Robert McAfee Brown, *P. T. Forsyth: Prophet for Today* (Philadelphia: Westminster Press, 1952), p. 27.

[6]P. T. Forsyth, *Positive Preaching and the Modern Mind*, p. 89.

[7]Ibid., p. 133.

[8]P. T. Forsyth, *The Church and the Sacraments* (London: Independent Press Ltd., 1947), p. 18.

[9]Arthur C. Cochrane, *The Church's Confession Under Hitler* (Philadelphia: Westminster Press, 1962), p. 239.

[10]Here I am using *catholicism* in the sense of an evangelical catholicism, the true catholic faith that is wider and deeper than Roman or Anglo-Catholicism.

Chapter 7

[1]See Heinz Zahrnt, *The Historical Jesus*, trans. J. S. Bowden (New York: Harper & Row, 1963), p. 49.

[2]Richard Wurmbrand, *Christ in the Communist Prisons*, ed. Charles Foley (New York: Coward-McCann, Inc., 1968), p. 46.

[3]She eventually recovered and became a genuine partner in her husband's ministry, though she remained on the home front.

[4]Norman P. Grubb, *C. T. Studd* (Fort Washington, Pa: Christian Literature Crusade, n.d.), p. 212.

[5]Ibid., pp. 165-66.

[6]P. T. Forsyth, *The Justification of God* (London: Independent Press Ltd., 1948), p. 220.

[7]Dietrich Bonhoeffer, *Ethics*, ed. Eberhard Bethge, trans. Neville Horton Smith (New York: Macmillan Co., 1965), p. 81.

Chapter 8

[1]Martin Luther, *Preface to the Epistle to the Romans* in *Works of Martin Luther*, Vol. VI, trans. C. M. Jacobs (Philadelphia: A. J. Holman Co., 1932), p. 451.

[2]*John Wesley*, Albert C. Outler, ed. (New York: Oxford Univ. Press, 1964), p. 66.

Scripture Index

Subject Index

Name Index